* * *

"Ever since the Emperor Constantine sought conformity of faith across the Roman Empire by imposing fixed doctrinal understandings, a more foundational Christian narrative, fluid, imaginative and subversive, has been suppressed. In this book, Peter Keenan, invoking the ancient wisdom of midrash, recaptures what Christianity looked like before it became so rigidly institutionalized. The reader is presented with an enlightened view of this ancient wisdom - which remarkably affirms and reinforces the liberating wisdom pursued by many spiritual seekers in the 21st Century."

Diarmuid O'Murchu
Specialises in Adult Faith Development, author of
When the Disciple Comes of Age (2019)

* * *

The Birth of Jesus the Jew

Midrash and the Infancy Gospels

PETER KEENAN

columba
BOOKS

First published in 2021 by
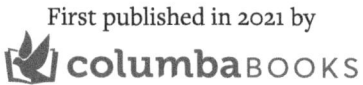

Block 3b, Bracken Business Park,
Bracken Road, Sandyford, Dublin 18, D18 K277
www.columbabooks.com

Copyright © 2021 Peter Keenan

All rights reserved. Without limiting the rights under copyright reserved alone, no part of this publication may be reproduced, stored in or introduced into a retrieval system, or transmitted, in any form or by any means (electronic, mechanical, photocopying, recording or otherwise) without the prior written permission of both the copyright owner and the above publisher of the book.

ISBN: 978-1-78218-382-2

Set in Freight Text Pro and Freight Sans Pro 11.5/15.5
Cover and book design by Alba Esteban | Columba Books

Frontcover image:
Watercolour illustration © 'Mary, Joseph and Donkey'
by Thomas Plunkett PPRWS.

Printed by ScandBook, Falun.

ABOUT THE AUTHOR

PETER KEENAN was born in Dublin. He studied for the priesthood but left before ordination. He holds a B. A. degree in Theology specialising in history and religious studies. Peter has lectured extensively at gatherings for clergy, students, laity and teachers.

In 1986, Peter was appointed an adviser to the Catholic Bishops' Conference of England and Wales. He served for many years as secretary to its Committee for Catholic-Jewish Relations. Peter has led educational visits/pilgrimages to the Holy Land. He describes himself as a post-Holocaust Catholic.

Contents

Dedication – 9

Acknowledgements – 13

Chapter 1
From Death to Birth: An Introduction – 15

Chapter 2
Born and lived in Nazareth of Galilee – 25

Chapter 3
A Tale of Two Virgins – 35

Chapter 4
Heroes of Divine Origin – 47

Chapter 5
The Queen of Sheba Visits Bethlehem – 57

Chapter 6
Better to be Herod's Pig than Herod's Son – 67

Chapter 7
A Problem Child – 77

In Place of a Conclusion – 87

Endnotes – 93

Dedication

The Birth of Jesus the Jew (BJJ), which makes no claim to originality, is dedicated with profound gratitude to the devoted and caring majority of Irish sisters, brothers and priests without whom I and millions of other children would not have had an education.

The scandals exposed in recent years – and rightly excoriated – must not be allowed to detract from their sincere, sometimes heroic, efforts to benefit young people. The vocation of those who were nurses and doctors is also recognised in this dedication.

It is further dedicated to the parishioners of St John Fisher Catholic parish, North West London, who engaged graciously, bemusedly and enthusiastically with a series of twelve 'lectures' (*Theology on Tap*), one of which was 'No Star of Bethlehem' (Advent 2016).

As a post-Holocaust Catholic, and to paraphrase Robert Funk, I believe that the sterile theological squabbling between Christian denominations needs to be replaced by a frank and radical appraisal of Jesus the Jew in the context of his times, liberated from 'the scriptural and creedal prisons in which we have incarcerated him'.[1]

The Gospel of Jesus needs to be distinguished from the Jesus of the Gospels and to be permitted to speak for itself, in so far as such an ideal is attainable 2,000 years after this remarkable man's death and resurrection.

We cannot go back to the first century and 'translate' some idealised version of it for our circumstances, a flaw – however worthy its purpose – in much of the late nineteenth century's approach to 'Jesus Studies', which continued well into the twentieth century, until Geza Vermes' ground-breaking *Jesus the Jew* was published in 1973. Years later, it awakened me from my 'dogmatic simplicities', to paraphrase Kant. A Jew and former Catholic priest, Vermes (d. 2013) has transformed my understanding of Jesus, a process that began one night in a Carmelite friary in 1975.

This book recognises that the academic quest for the historical Jesus should not determine, but it can influence for the better, how Christianity is to be lived today, for the simple reason that Judaism and Christianity are now separate and – before God – legitimate religions in their own right (I subscribe to the 'two covenant' position).

The effective failure of Christians down the centuries to acknowledge this seminal truth resulted in great suffering for the descendants of Jesus the Jew, born in Nazareth.

One problem, our Christian shame, is that, since the second century, when many Jewish scholars pointed to major inconsistencies in the emerging Christian Narrative, including its Passion and Birth Stories (the latter were written after the former), nascent Christianity ignored these objections. In time, that moral failure contributed unwittingly to the Holocaust.

Acknowledgements

Peter de Rosa has remarked that 'Knowledge does not always bring wisdom; ignorance never does'. For any wisdom that readers may discover in this slim volume, thanks is owed to many people, too numerous to list; but where any ignorance may remain, the fault is entirely mine.

I wish to acknowledge nonetheless the sustained, good-humoured assistance of three 'agony uncles' – Hugh Barriscale, Paul Hewitt and Paul Higginson – and of one 'agony aunt' – Alexandra Archer.

Without them, it is unlikely that this book would have seen the light of day, and almost certainly not its soon-to-be published (much lengthier) sequel – The Death of Jesus the Jew: Midrash & Gospel Truth in the Shadow of the Holocaust.

In addition, much appreciated is the editorial assistance provided by Dr Niamh Prior and Mrs Rosamund Cargin, in respect of both books when in draft form, and the guidance and encouragement provided by Garry O'Sullivan and his team at Columba Books.

Take care and watch yourselves closely, do not forget the things your eyes have seen, nor let them slip from your memory all the days of your life; make them known to your children, and to your children's children.

(DEUTERONOMY 4:9, REDACTED)

CHAPTER 1

From Death to Birth: An Introduction

He was created of a mother whom he created.
he was carried by hands that he formed.
he cried in the manger in wordless infancy.
he, the word,
without whom all human eloquence is mute.

(ST AUGUSTINE, D. 430)

Jesus and Queen Elizabeth II share an odd distinction. She has two birthdays – the official one in June when she troops the colour and her real one, 21 April; Jesus has two birthplaces – the official one, Bethlehem, and the real one, Nazareth.

The four Passion Narratives and the two Infancy Narratives of the Gospel are primarily faith testimonies about the historicisation of prophecy, having little to do with 'remembered history', to paraphrase John Dominic Crossan.

They are largely the product of *midrashim* (explained below), which is how Jesus has come to have two birthplaces, and it is most likely also the reason why the evangelists tell us that, on the day of his crucifixion (probably 7 April 30 CE), his body was laid in a tomb hewn out of rock provided by Joseph of Arimathea (Mark 15:42–47 and parallels).

This story was almost certainly inspired by Isaiah 53:9 – 'They made his grave with the wicked and his tomb with the rich, although he had done no violence, and there was no deceit in his mouth' (see Matthew 27:57).

Jesus' corpse, assuming it was not left on the cross as carrion, was most probably laid in a communal pit, a common first-century Roman practice: 'With regard to the body of Jesus, by Easter morning, those who cared did not know where it was, and those who knew did not care.'[2]

The Passion Narratives in particular were the unintended seedbed for the notorious Teaching of Contempt (see Chapter 6). In time, it provided the basis for the racial anti-Semitism of the nineteenth century and it paved the road to the Holocaust.

It must be emphasised that the four evangelists and other New Testament authors were not promoting what is sometimes termed Christian anti-Semitism, nor were they writing fiction in the manner in which we understand it. The New Testament is an honest account of their interpretation of Jesus, written employing different literary genres, cognisant of the reality that religious insights do not have to conform to a simplistic equation between 'fact' and 'truth'.

There is, however, anti-Judaism in the New Testament, reflecting both the extraordinary circumstances prevailing after the Great Jewish Roman War (66–70/73) and a genre of Jewish polemical literature that is also found in the 'Old Testament'.

The Shoah is nonetheless Christianity's greatest tragedy, the culmination of centuries of anti-Jewish polemic rooted in prejudice, ignorance and very bad theology.

Jules Isaac's *The Teaching of Contempt* (1964) notes that,

from the latter third of the first century, the Christian Church proclaimed that:

- The destruction of the Temple (70) and the subsequent collapse of the Jewish state was a consequence of God's punishment for the Jews' putative rejection of Jesus.
- Judaism of the first century was degenerate and in terminal decline.
- The Jewish people 'murdered God'.[3]

There is an account of a conversation with a papal nuncio in 1944, at the height of the Holocaust, in which he is reported to have said, 'There is no innocent blood of Jewish children in the world. All Jewish blood is guilty. You have to die. This is the punishment that has been awaiting you because of the sin of deicide.'[4]

St Matthew recounts Herod's murder of innocent children at the time of Jesus' birth (Matthew 2:16–18). Some academics interpret the story to be an early form of Supersessionism, the claim that Christianity replaced Judaism. Its historical context, however, is that Matthew has crafted a piece of brilliant midrash, based on the account in Exodus 1:15–2:10 of Pharaoh's attempt to kill the infant Moses. Pharaoh is now 'Herod' and Jesus is the 'new Moses'.

Matthew's account contributed inadvertently to the papal nuncio's ludicrous claim that 'All Jewish blood is guilty', which arose from the notorious Teaching of Contempt. The nuncio had no awareness of midrash.

The Hebrew word *midrash* signifies an interpretation of the past applied to subsequent contemporary situations, where accounts in the Bible provide the original context for later narratives. Micah 5:2 – 'But you, O Bethlehem ... from you shall come forth for me one who is to rule Israel' – typifies this phenomenon. It provides one of the incentives for situating Jesus' birth in Bethlehem, about fifty-five years after his death and resurrection.

The origins of midrash can be traced back to the Jews' Exile in Babylon in the sixth century BCE, when they searched their sacred writings to give meaning to the fate that had befallen them. Hubert Richards has explained how this methodology gave rise to an entirely new tradition. It was not so much a rereading, but a retelling, of the Bible, 'in which old texts were re-written to make them applicable and relevant to new situations'.[5] In other words, 'the past throws light on the present'.[6]

A.N. Wilson has written that the New Testament, particularly its Birth and Passion Narratives, is 'soaked in Midrash'. As a literary form it is certainly strange, and Richards uses an analogy from the construction industry to elucidate how it works: 'Old materials are used in the building of new structures, meaning that what is being discussed is always in one sense a *present event*, but it is articulated in terms borrowed from the past.'[7]

It is in the light of these considerations that we should understand the composition of the New Testament's two Infancy Narratives, including Luke 2:41–52 (the boy Jesus in the Temple). These accounts provide us with no biographical, historical or biological information.[8] The Infancy Narratives are instances of *haggadic midrashim* (interpretation of stories or events by relating them to other stories and events, which is how, for example, the Massacre of the Innocents came to be written).

These stories, however, are genuine faith testimonies, reflecting a stage towards the end of the first century when

Greek-speaking Jewish Christians in the Diaspora had become convinced that Jesus had been constituted Messiah from his conception. Aramaic-speaking Jewish Christians, on the other hand, believed that Jesus would become the Messiah at the end of the world.[9]

When sceptics point to the obvious discrepancies in, and contradictions between, the Infancy Narratives, they miss the point. It should not worry us, for example, that St Luke knew nothing about the Flight into Egypt and that St Matthew had no awareness of an angelic chorus on that Silent Night, for the simple reason that there was no Silent Night. The evangelists had no problem with such inconsistencies because 'these stories are primarily exercises in creative *midrashim*, their object being to show that Jesus' coming was foretold in the Hebrew Scriptures'.[10]

Matthew and Luke knew they were writing a type of what nowadays we term 'hagiography', and not history, in the sense that it has come to be understood in the modern world, which too often assumes that something is true only if it is at the same time factual, a phenomenon sometimes referred to as fact-fundamentalism. The writers of the New Testament had no truck with this approach, now the preserve of Christian fundamentalisms of various complexions and their unlikely bedfellow: fundamentalist atheism.

Biblical literalism has a complex history, but one Christian academic put his finger on the problem when he identified it as 'a Gentile heresy'. Scriptural fundamentalism arises from an inability to respect on its own terms the religion of Jesus the Jew and its continuing, vibrant growth since his lifetime, for the reason that, from early in the second century, 'Gentile Christianity' began to lose contact with its roots in the Jesus Movement.[11]

Christian fundamentalists, despite what they proclaim to the contrary, are unable to embrace 'the religious imagination', to borrow a famous phrase of Aristotle that he applied to the ethical life.

The New Testament is the product of fallible religious imagination(s). As such, it exhibits the strengths and weaknesses inherent in the struggle to apprehend divine realities. There is much truth in the observation that it was authored in consequence of the cognitive dissonance experienced by believers when Jesus failed to return, and the Infancy Narratives clearly reflect that concern. They highlight a phase midway in the development of New Testament Christology between Jesus' original status as 'Son of Man' and his ultimate eminence as 'Divine Son of God'.[12]

This book maintains that, whilst there is no requirement for Christians to subscribe to a literalist reading of the Infancy Narratives (that the Holy Family fled to Egypt, for example), it nonetheless repudiates claims that Jesus never existed. It is one thing to say that Jesus was born in Nazareth, but it is of an entirely different order to assert that he was not born at all. This is the position advocated by Thomas Brodie, the eminent biblical scholar and former Dominican priest.

In his *Memoir of a Discovery*, he writes:

> Outside of the classroom I scarcely ever alluded to having a particular view of the way the biblical texts were composed and, when preaching at weekends in a parish, I was usually able to concentrate on the message of the text without becoming involved in problems of history. In fact, leaving history aside generally made it easier to deal with the meaning. However, when

conversations developed about the Bible, it was often difficult to avoid questions of history, and one woman in the parish began to realise there was something I was not saying. She and her family became my friends, but still I hedged and hedged, dreading what I would do to her faith if I told her what I thought, and the fear of damaging her encapsulated the fear of what I would do to so many other people. One night while visiting, she and I were sitting alone on the living room couch... , and the conversation turned to my work, and she asked what most concerned me about the Bible. Eventually I said, 'It's about Jesus.' I was physically holding myself together, looking down at the carpet: 'He never really existed.'

Brodie's friend (a parishioner of Tallaght, County Dublin) replied, 'Oh, that's what I believed since I was a little girl.'[13] She was a precocious child – weren't we all!

Brodie's thesis, and it has much to commend it, is that the primary literary model behind the New Testament is the biblical account of Elijah and Elisha (an observation made by the late Raymond Brown as far back as 1971), but it seems extraordinary to maintain also that Jesus never existed.

A.N. Wilson has identified a major problem with the argument. Brodie fails to give sufficient attention to the fact that not all of the New Testament fits into a previous template, because 'not every moment of the Gospels is a Midrash on older scripture – though amazing numbers of them are.'[14]

Wilson notes that this criticism is particularly relevant to the Passion Narratives, maintaining that Simon of Cyrene, more likely than not, is a historical figure. Wilson somewhat overstates the critique, failing to recognise that if Barabbas, for instance, is a narrative device (as he almost certainly is), then Simon of Cyrene falls into the same category.

Brodie concedes that the weakest part of his theory is to provide a satisfactory explanation for why, from its inception, the Jesus Movement insisted upon the fact of Jesus' crucifixion ('resurrection' does not worry him; he argues that the 'appearances' derive largely from the Book of Numbers).

He asserts that crucifixion, *the* method of Roman state terrorism at the time, best represents the evangelists' efforts to identify their literary Jesus as one who is associated with the oppressed, patterned on the famous Suffering Servant and other passages, represented by 'a clear contemporary image – Roman crucifixion'.[15]

St Mark's Passion Narrative was largely based on Old Testament narratives – the notorious 'Judas kiss', for example – yet it nonetheless preserved some historical memories, in particular the fact of Jesus' crucifixion, notwithstanding the consideration that it was narrated in terms of liturgy masquerading as history (the 'Pilate trial', for instance, is not historical, contrary to Raymond Brown's claim to 'verisimilitude').[16] A perfunctory acquaintance with Good Friday liturgies supports this observation.

Contrary to Brodie's position, Jesus was a real human being, born in Nazareth, who ministered (almost) exclusively in the Galilee for at least six months (29–30). Jesus was a loyal son of the covenant. The religion about him, whose foundation he inspired, is Christianity.

An argument can be made for his death having occurred in late 29, which was then interpreted about seven months later against the background of Passover – the high point of the Jewish liturgical year. It is a hypothesis favouring Brodie's theory. In the final analysis, however, the overall theory, whilst being persuasive, does not convince, but he certainly encourages us to read the Bible with new eyes.

Wilson also makes the acute observation that the Bible has not had a life separate from the lives of ordinary people, but that Christian fundamentalists want to make 'the true organic living Bible into an ersatz Bible like the Book of Mormon'.[17]

The implication is that we grant too much privilege to what at first sight appears to be 'history' in the interpretation of sacred texts, not to mention the fact that when the authors of these narratives composed their work they were not particularly concerned with notions like 'doctrine', 'inspiration' and 'revelation', notwithstanding the claim of 2 Timothy 3:16 that 'all scripture is inspired by God, and it is useful for teaching' (abridged).

Has God really 'inspired' the words: 'Let his blood be upon us and on our children' (Matthew 27:25)? The verse has been described by Benedict Viviano, a Dominican scholar, as 'bitter, polemical and ugly', the words of human beings, having nothing to do with God or Jesus.[18]

The central message of the Hebrew and Christian Bibles is that God is a 'verb', not a 'noun', meaning that he is constantly emerging into our world as one who challenges us to embrace a future of hope, one that is not circumscribed by adherence to outdated dogmatisms.[19]

John Maynard Keynes said, 'When the facts change, I change my mind'. In Ireland, Tony Flannery, a former Redemptorist priest who speaks truth to power, is a courageous and prophetic embodiment of Keynes's maxim. He knows, as do other 'wise elders' (to borrow a term from Diarmuid O'Murchu), that 'Catholic imperialism has no clothes' (this observation does not apply to Catholicism's excellent theology of grace, properly understood).

Flannery, in his engaging *From the Outside – Rethinking Church Dogmas*, quotes Pierre Teilhard de Chardin (d.1955), who identified three of the 'weakest stones' in the foundations of the modern Church, one of which is its refusal to engage with 'a revelation that excludes future prophecy'.[20] In this regard, Flannery, probably unwittingly, reflects an observation of Immanuel Kant (d. 1804), in his famous essay 'Answer the Question: What is Enlightenment?', where he argues that appeals to 'Christian founders' should not be allowed to impede the onward development of religion.

Kant's writings were placed on the notorious Index of Forbidden Books, and Flannery has encountered a contemporary manifestation of the prohibition. The problem lies with the Index, not with Tony Flannery, who is driving forward without a neurotic attachment to rearview-mirror theology.

We need to find more creative and humble ways of adapting our biblical and theological narratives to contemporary realities, if St Augustine's beautiful words about Jesus, 'without whom all human eloquence is mute', are to flourish anew in Christian discourse after the Holocaust. This book is a contribution to that endeavour. From death there sometimes comes new birth and that is how, about two generations after Jesus' crucifixion, these moving words came to be written:

> I am bringing you good news of great joy for all the people – to you is born this day, in the city of David, a Saviour, who is the Messiah, the Lord.
> (LUKE 2:10–11)

CHAPTER 2
—
Born and Lived in Nazareth of Galilee

*Jesus knew that he was not born
in Bethlehem of Judaea.*

Jesus was born not in 'David's city' but in Nazareth, towards the end of the era known as Second Temple Judaism (536 BCE–70/73 CE). We have no way of identifying definitively the year and month, but an educated guess is that it was probably 4 BCE. The genealogies of the Gospels of Matthew and Luke provide us with no historical data. Their purpose is to present Jesus as the fulfilment of Israel's hope (Matthew) and the claim that he is universal saviour (Luke).

Christmas as a distinctive liturgical feast seems not to have been celebrated before about 330. In the Eastern Church, Epiphany has always been more important. Our contemporary celebration of Christmas has much to do with nineteenth-century sentimentality, promoted by Prince Albert and Charles Dickens.

25 December was actually believed to be the birthday of Mithras, a mythical Persian sun god, allegedly born in a cave – of a virgin mother and a divine father. Our 'Sunday' may reflect the

popularity of his cult. This mystery religion was favoured by Roman soldiers and, for a time there was the unlikely possibility that it, and not Christianity, might have become the state religion of the empire. A shrine to Mithras was discovered close to the Bank of England in London in 1954.

Arguments favouring Jesus' birth in Bethlehem labour under multiple disadvantages, including that there is no reference to it in the seven genuine letters of St Paul, our first known Christian writer, nor in St Mark's Gospel.[21] Paul writes in Romans that Jesus was born 'from the seed of David according to the flesh' (Romans 1:3), and it is this claim that has provided one of the influences for situating it in Bethlehem, to provide Jesus with 'Davidic credentials'. It is an excellent instance of how midrash works: building blocks are taken from one context and applied to a new set of circumstances.

Jesus knew that he was not born in 'Bethlehem of Judaea'. It is the birthplace of the Christ.[22] Growing up in Galilee, Jesus was part of a vibrant political, religious and social world and, according to one hypothesis, there is the possibility that he was trilingual, speaking Aramaic, Hebrew and some Greek.

This hypothesis is based on the assumption that Jesus worked as a craftsman in Sepphoris, a Jewish-Hellenistic city about five kilometres from Nazareth. There is no way of confirming this claim. It has the merit, however, of reminding us that, contrary to some views, the historical Jesus may have had more interaction with Gentiles than has been previously thought. This might explain why, so soon after his death and resurrection, the Jesus Movement had gained influence in the synagogues of the Diaspora, particularly those of Antioch and Damascus. (It was at Antioch that the disciples were first called 'Christians'– see Acts 11: 26.)

It would seem that St Paul's 'conversion' occurred in such a context (see Acts 9:1-22), but contrary to popular opinion he never envisaged the establishment of a new religion: 'Paul did not become a Christian because there were no Christians at that time.'[23] It is a misconception that bedevils Christianity to this day and it has within living memory contributed indirectly to the horror that is the Holocaust.

St Paul argued that Christ had become the pathway to salvation for Gentiles. Despite what many Christians think, he did not believe Jesus to be God, notwithstanding certain passages in the genuine letters (Philippians 2:6-11, The Hymn to Christ, for example) and later epistles attributed to him (of course, this does not mean that Jesus is *not* God).

Paul envisages similarity rather than identity when he compares Jesus (the Christ) to God.[24] He proclaims beliefs rather than explaining them, typified by the claim that 'God was in Christ' (Romans 8:38), and this may point to his conviction that Jesus had some kind of pre-existence status.

Paul never endorsed the abrogation of Torah for Jews, regardless of how some of his writings – displaced from their original context – may appear to support this interpretation, no more than he envisaged a world without the Temple. His objection was to Gentile ('Christian') believers practising Torah, for which he saw no need, with particular regard to circumcision, a quite literal embodiment of the covenant between God and Abraham. It is fallacious to argue that Paul preached a law-free gospel: the Jesus Movement, even before him, admitted Gentile converts without requiring them to be circumcised.

James (the brother of Jesus) and Peter, in the Jerusalem Church, endorsed this position, but – with Paul – they still required converts to worship exclusively the God of Israel, to refrain from fornication and not to partake of food offered to idols. In other words, they were expected to conform to key tenets of Torah.

It would be a mistake to postulate an ideological chasm between James and Paul, notwithstanding the famous dispute related in 2 Galatians 11:14. These verses reflect the claim of the 'false brethren' that Jesus' return had been delayed because converts in the Diaspora refused to be circumcised (Galatians 2:4). When Jesus was boy and adult, these concerns were not part of his religious worldview, but they kick-started the religion that bears his 'surname', and that is why we should be aware of them, even if this book is largely about 'Christmas'.

If, following the crucifixion, the disciples had not had an 'Easter Experience', none of us, in the twenty-first century, would be tucking into Christmas dinner on 25 December; only much later did there emerge the need to invent Christmas, a 'birthday' unknown to the historical Jesus. Christmas, as the name suggests, is all about 'the Christ', not Jesus.[25]

Jesus probably lived most of his life in Nazareth, a small town in Galilee, and it would seem that his ministry was directed chiefly at villages of the Lower Galilee, with a few visits to Jerusalem. He may also have ministered briefly across from the Jordan River.

Despite the fact that this was a turbulent time when the Jews yearned for liberation from their latest oppressor, the Romans, Galilee – under the delegated rule of Herod Antipas from 4 BCE to 39 CE – remained peaceful, with one major exception in 6 CE that affected the entire region. It was occasioned indirectly by Quirinius, the military governor of the area who ruled for three years. (Varus was the actual governor of Syria.)

Judaea was a very different kettle of fish because Jerusalem was a magnet for political and religious agitation. Archelaus, the other surviving son of Herod the Great (d. 4 BCE), who ruled Judaea under Roman sufferance, inherited most of his father's disreputable character traits.

Archelaus's reign was a disaster, ending in 6 CE when Augustus, the emperor, banished him to Gaul (roughly modern-day France) because of gross misgovernment, which caused Judaea to be incorporated into the province of Syria. That same year Quirinius ordered the first Roman census of what later came to be called 'Palestine'. It came as a bitter shock to the Jews, and the resulting higher levels of taxation caused a rebellion, led by Judas the Galilean, who interpreted the measure as an offence against God. The insurrection was brutally suppressed by the Romans.

Archelaus features briefly in Matthew's Infancy Narrative (2:22), but his real claim to fame is that Rome thereafter appointed procurators to govern Judaea, the most famous of whom is Pontius Pilate (26–36), during whose tenure Jesus was executed.

It is ironic that Pilate was also relieved of his office because of his mismanagement of a crisis to do with a Samaritan village, which he wiped out, having mistaken a religious gathering for an act of revolt. One legend has it that he was executed by Nero. A different account, perhaps more accurate, is that he died in Vienna. Either way, we know far more about Pilate's life – that he married the granddaughter of Augustus, for instance – than we know about the historical Jesus.

The late Sean Freyne (d. 2013) explained why some academics have designated the region 'Galilee of the Gentiles'. Their argument is that Galileans were more exposed than other Jews to Greek and Roman culture ('Hellenism'), thereby embracing a more open form of Judaism.[26]

Freyne observes that this perspective – that Galilee was more pagan than Jewish – is poorly attested by literary sources and receives no support from archaeological explorations. It reached a virulent crescendo with Walter Grundmann's assertion in 1941 that because 'Galilee was pagan' Jesus was in all probability not Jewish. The preposterous claim is the likely basis for Hitler's allegation, reported after the Second World War in various accounts of his *Tischgespräche* (Hitler's private conversations in the period 1941–44), that a Roman legionary from Gaul was the father of Jesus.

Celsus (d. 186), a pagan philosopher, objected to the developing belief about Jesus' divinity and accused Mary of having had an adulterous relationship with 'Panthera', the 'legionary from Gaul'. The name is a likely pun on 'parthenos', Matthew's term for 'virgin', which Celsus probably got from a Jewish source.[27]

It is worth observing that, from a theoretical first-century Jewish perspective, 'Mary's virginity *ante partum* (before Jesus' birth) was not rejected on the grounds that such a conception is beyond the means of an omnipotent God'.[28] The point is that even a miraculous pregnancy does not mean that the child born thereof is 'God Incarnate'.

Many books, ancient and modern, have been written about Jesus' so-called 'hidden years'. They are complete fictions. We know nothing about him prior to c. 29, and even then, our knowledge is mediated through the prism of faith testimonies.

The evangelists had no knowledge of, and little interest in, the place of Jesus' birth. Their concern was not with *when* and *how* and *where*, but with w*ho he is*.[29] What mattered to them was not Mary's biological status but the destiny of her son. For these reasons, it is misguided to attempt a harmonisation of the two canonical Infancy Gospels. Matthew and Luke were not diarists in the mould of Samuel Pepys (d. 1703), who chronicled the Great Fire of London.

After the birth, Luke has the family return to Nazareth and Matthew has them fleeing to Egypt, migrating later to Nazareth (see Luke 2:39-40 and Matthew 2:1-12). Both accounts cannot be historical and the truth is that neither is factual. The *why* of Jesus' life, understood c. 80, is what mattered to Matthew and Luke, and they articulated that significance as 'parable', not history.

A grandmother-to-be does not sit in a maternity unit awaiting the birth of a famous grandson, not that such considerations would prevent her from worrying about her daughter's prolonged labour. Søren Kierkegaard (d. 1855) observes that 'Life is lived forwards but understood backwards.' Infancy stories about famous religious people are always exercises in hagiography. It is true of the Buddha and it is true of Jesus.

The Buddha reputedly assumed the form of a white elephant and went to where his soon-to-be mother was protected by guardian angels. He struck her side with his trunk, thereby 'entering her womb'. It is noteworthy that, at his subsequent birth, the 'heavenly host' rejoiced in celebration of it. A slightly different version of the legend has the Buddha's mother, Queen Maya, dreaming about the elephant, which subsequently became her son, with the help of a lotus flower, and at his birth four angels received the baby in a golden net.

Every December, primary school teachers usually produce nativity plays. These brave undertakings, imaginative adaptations of the Infancy Narratives, invite us to celebrate 'good news of great joy for all the people' (Luke 2:10b). With due respect to the Buddha and elephants, it is a mercy that teachers can get away with donkeys and wise men without having to include elephants in their creative pastiches.

The Buddha's earliest followers looked for allegorical and symbolic meaning in the elephant story. They did not interpret it literally, and later biographies of the Buddha include mythological stories about the 'earth shaking' and the 'opening of gates', echoing themes in the much later New Testament (see Matthew 27:51b and Acts 12:6–19).

We Christians should acknowledge humbly that the Infancy Narratives convey profound religious meaning and need to be understood in the context of Jesus' death and resurrection, which made possible the composition of the birth stories; there would have been no 'Bethlehem' without Golgotha.

There is no requirement, however, to force these narratives into the straitjacket of 'fact' and 'history', let alone 'biology', in the sense that such terms are typically understood in our post-Enlightenment world. Thus, in the paraphrased words of A.N. Wilson, 'Matthew' and 'Luke' started out with a set of beliefs about Jesus and shaped their narratives in the light of those beliefs, not the other way round.

The birth stories utilise *midrashim*, 'parable' and symbols, the only means available to Luke, for example, when he proclaimed, 'Glory to God in the highest heaven, and on Earth peace amongst those whom He favours' (2:14).

When Christians today reflect upon the significance of 'good news of great joy for all the people', it should be a moral imperative – in the shadows cast by the Holocaust – to reflect upon how that 'good news' in its original context referred not to what has become a disaster and rescue story about the redemption of the entire world, but rather to the story of Israel: 'I will make of you a great nation' (Genesis 12:2a).[30]

For understandable reasons, we interpret the Infancy Narratives with regard to four essential beliefs of the Christian narrative:

- ▶ Creation
- ▶ Fall
- ▶ Redemption effected through Christ and
- ▶ Consummation of all things when his expected return occurs

The supposed Fall of Humankind, for example, scarcely figures in Jewish tradition, and outside of Genesis 3 it appears nowhere else in the Hebrew Bible.[31] This myth is the basis for the Christian doctrine of Original Sin, developed by St Augustine, and it has had some disastrous consequences both for Western civilisation in general and for the Jewish people in particular.

There is much to recommend the view that Christians of the twenty-first century need to modify this fourfold scheme into a more historically aware and inclusive theology, articulating a double covenant approach to the relationship between Judaism and Christianity. This recognises without equivocation that God wills at least two equal ways of relating to him.

Late Second Temple Judaism, after its defeat in the Great Jewish-Roman War, gave birth to two daughters – what we now recognise as normative Judaism and Christianity – and these sisters owe much to the teaching of the Pharisees.

The diatribe against them in Matthew 23 bears about as much resemblance to historical reality as the claim that Jesus was taken down alive from the Cross, migrated to India and fathered children there.

The one-covenant approach advocated by Catholicism maintains that Gentiles are admitted to it by virtue of Christ, and that ultimately Jews will be reconciled to that reality (see Romans 11:25–26). This book goes further, endorsing the prophetic conviction of the late Jonathan Sacks (d. 2020):

> The God of Abraham is the Father of all humankind, but the faith of Abraham is not the religion of all humankind.[32]

It is in this context that we should approach Luke's 'good news of great joy for all the people', which was not always good news for the Jews.

We sentimentalise the Infancy Narratives, ignoring their dark side, forgetting that they mirror the Passion Narratives, written in the light of Judaism's First Great Catastrophe.

CHAPTER 3

—

A Tale of Two Virgins

A young woman is with child.

In 66, Jews energised by the party of the Zealots supported an insurrection against Rome. It caused the destruction of the Temple and, in 73, on the mountaintop fortress at Masada, the 900 remaining insurrectionists chose suicide rather than surrender to the enemy, bringing to an end the First Great Jewish-Roman War. The second one was from 132 to 135, after which the Jewish state was effectively 'dead', and wouldn't re-emerge until after the Second World War.

Historians estimate that, in terms of estimated percentage of population, more Jews died during that First War than perished in the Holocaust, albeit for very different reasons. It is impossible to overstate the significance of the destruction of the Temple, fifteen storeys high (craftsmen were still working on its enlargement literally days before disaster struck on 9 August 70).

When Luke says, 'Do not be afraid, Zechariah, for your prayer has been heard, Elizabeth will bear you a son, and you will name him John' (1:13), he was writing in the light of a back-story – that First War. The name John means 'God has been gracious'.

No better example of that graciousness, save one (the virginal conception), is that barren Elizabeth, whose pregnancy has been disclosed to Mary by the Angel Gabriel, enables her to say about her own condition, in the Magnificat, that God has brought down 'the powerful from their thrones and lifted up the lowly' (1:52). It is an obvious midrash on Hannah's Prayer in 1 Samuel 2:1–10: 'The Lord makes poor and makes rich; he brings low, he also exalts' (v.8). The Rosary's Joyful Mysteries are effectively a meditation on these ten verses.

An interesting feature of the Magnificat is that it reflects political ideas expressed by women elsewhere in the Hebrew Bible, a theme developed by Luke.[33] We see it most clearly in the affirmation that 'to you is born this day in the city of David a Saviour, who is the Messiah' (2:11). He is making the point that, notwithstanding the outcome of the First Great Jewish-Roman War, emerging Gentile Christianity had adopted the position that the Christ, not Caesar, stands at the centre and true meaning of the history of the known world.

It was a breathtaking claim, one that eventually culminated in the affirmation at Chalcedon (451) – that 'Jesus is true God and true man'. Christians often assume that this understanding was more or less present from the beginning of the Jesus Movement, but Chalcedon was slow to develop against the background of complex political, social and philosophical considerations.

Many Jewish-Christians, typified by the Ebionites, refused to accept the belief. Known also as the Nazarenes (James, the brother of Jesus, was probably of their number), they survived in some form – ostracised by rabbinic Judaism and 'Catholicism' – into the fifth century.

The Ebionites were convinced of Jesus' prophetic and messianic status, but they rejected utterly any suggestion that he was somehow 'divine'. This rejection was similar to their disapproval of Paul, whom they regarded as a 'false prophet'.[34]

It is unsurprising that the Nazarenes were sceptical of how Matthew 1:23 came to be understood:

> Look, the virgin shall conceive and bear a son, and they shall name him Emmanuel.

It is probably one of the verses most familiar to Christians and yet it is much misunderstood. About 260 BCE, according to legend, King Ptolemy II of Egypt wanted a copy of the Torah for his famous library in Alexandria. Seventy scholars are said to have got to work producing a Greek translation of the Hebrew Scriptures, known as the Septuagint (LXX). It is this text that was chiefly availed of by the New Testament's authors, but there are many discrepancies between it and the original Hebrew version(s).[35]

Isaiah 7:14 is the most famous discrepancy, which is copied at Matthew 1:23. Later editions of the LXX corrected the error, after Matthew's Gospel was written. The original Hebrew verse reads: 'Look, the young woman is with child and shall bear a son, and shall name him Emmanuel.' Its use of a different tense is very significant.

We should interpret Matthew's use of Greek Isaiah against the background of fulfilment citations (known also as proof texts). These are formulas used particularly in this gospel to introduce material related to Jesus: 'Joseph got up, took the child and his mother by night, and went to Egypt, and remained there until the death of Herod. This was to fulfil what had been spoken by the Lord through the prophet, "Out of Egypt I have called my son"' (Matthew 1:14–15). The citation is from Hosea 11:1.

An odd feature of these citations is that sometimes they do not exist. The reference at 2:23b, for example – that 'He will be called a Nazarene' – is found nowhere in the Jewish Scriptures, demonstrating the polemical nature of the citations in general. Their purpose – in the paraphrased words of Paula Fredriksen – is to provide biblical resonances for the evangelists' proclamation of Jesus as the Christ, and they were almost certainly adapted to liturgical contexts.

The citation from Hosea 11:1 is the basis for the story about the Flight into Egypt. It is an instance of midrash. A moment's reflection should convince us that, in the first century, a family of three is hardly likely to have undertaken such a journey – indeed, it would be highly irresponsible. Matthew is writing retrospective theology, not history, providing a back-story for Jesus' public ministry as the 'new Moses', which commences in Chapter 3 of his gospel, immediately after the manufactured Nazarene citation.

The quotation from Isaiah 7:14 serves a similar proclamatory function, an excellent illustration of prophecy historicised. We are so accustomed to interpreting this verse in the mistranslated version, with all of its later associations, that the original Hebrew context is either unknown or dismissed as irrelevant in the light of subsequent Christian beliefs about Jesus.

In 735 BCE, Ahaz, King of Judah, had a big problem. His capital, Jerusalem, was under siege from the armies of both Syria and the Northern Kingdom of Israel. In the midst of the siege, inspecting the battlements of the city's walls, 'he is confronted by the prophet Isaiah who informs him that Jerusalem will not fall to his enemies. Ahaz is unconvinced'.[36]

Isaiah then invites him to ask of God a confirmatory sign. Ahaz declines the invitation. He is then told that, regardless,

God will provide one: 'Behold, a young woman is with child' (Isaiah 7:14). The verse is a clear reference to Ahaz' wife, who gave birth to Hezekiah, the heir to the throne (Matthew 1:23 translates it as 'the virgin shall conceive and bear a son'). It is not a 'prophecy' about Jesus' conception, some 700 years later, which is a midrash on Ahaz' dilemma, translated into circumstances pertaining after another conflict: that First War, when famine effectively sealed Jerusalem's fate at the end of a long siege.

Ahaz and Isaiah were mercifully spared knowledge of that defeat, illustrated by the story of the fate of another baby, recounted by Simon Schama:

> Jerusalem is reduced to the last extremity. ... The nadir is reached with the story of a woman called Mary from across the Jordan and trapped in Jerusalem, reduced to such straits that she murders the baby boy sucking at her breast, roasts him and slices him in two, eating one half and setting the other aside for later.

She is discovered and, when the story gets round the city, those that are starving to death 'beg for the end', and those who are already dead 'are thought fortunate not to have survived to witness such things'.[37]

Matthew was unaware of this appalling story, but he most certainly was cognisant of Ahaz' dilemma, which provided him with the background for his use of Greek Isaiah 7:14, and it gave him a 'continuation theme' for one interpretation of Jewish existence after 70/73.

Hezekiah's birth thus represented the continuation of the Kingdom of Judah, and no more than that, having no association with 'virginity', rather like the chant in the Middle

Ages announcing a monarch's death: 'The king is dead, long live the king'.[38] The LXX translated 'young woman' (almah) as 'virgin' (parthenos), and the plain meaning of the former in its original context is that the young woman in question was not a virgin.

Geza Vermes argues convincingly that Matthew's account of Jesus' birth reflects an image of him born of a virgin and was designed with exclusive regard to Hellenistic Christianity.[39] This claim is supported by the evangelist's use of 'Emmanuel' (meaning 'God is with us', a phrase, not a proper name). It is a 'gloss' intended for the benefit of the gospel's non-Jewish Greek readers, with the connotation that the child had a supernatural nature and not merely a supernatural origin.

For the vast majority of Jews living in the Diaspora c. 80, and for those Palestinian Christians who may have had knowledge of an earlier, Aramaic version of this gospel, 'Emmanuel' could not have implied a 'supernatural nature'. 'Emmanuel', for them, meant simply a promise of help to the Jewish people, similar to Isaiah's prophecy directed at Ahaz.[40]

These observations lead to the deduction that the Hebrew text back-story of Greek Isaiah 7:14 does not prophesy the virginal conception of the Messiah, no more than the 'Old Testament' predicted one who would die a sacrificial death of atoning significance.

It has been argued that 'Christians, aware of the traditions of Jesus' unusual birth, discovered in Is. 7:14 a typological prophecy which found its ultimate fulfilment in Jesus, as Emmanuel.'[41] This book disputes that hypothesis. It was the other way round.

Isaiah 7:14 created the tradition about Jesus' unconventional birth, and the earliest (probably Aramaic) version of

Matthew's Gospel did not have this belief, contrary to a claim made by Mark L. Strauss: 'The virginal conception is not a late addition to the Gospel story.'[42] He is reflecting a theory that the belief may in some form antedate Mark's Gospel, written c. 70.

The truth is that the 'virginal conception' is the consequence of an error in the translation of Hebrew Isaiah 7:14. The editor of 'Aramaic Matthew' came across it as a lucky prophetic godsend. This enabled him 'to present to his Greek-speaking readers the birth of Jesus as unique, towering above all the other miraculous conceptions of the "Old Testament"'.[43]

It may be helpful at this point to say something about 'prophecy'. American law enforcement agencies in 1993 engaged for more than fifty days with a fundamentalist Christian sect in Waco, Texas. At the end of that engagement, eighty-six people were dead, including twenty-five children, some of whom may have been burned alive. The sect subscribed to the mantra 'What God says, He brings to pass', using verses primarily from the Book of Revelation to support its claims. It is a tragic example of the abuse of the concept, whereby 'prophecy' serves the interests of factional and dangerous elements in society, aiming to reshape reality in their image and likeness.

We have seen how Matthew 1:23, with its reference to a prophet's words, served as a fulfilment citation. Great care needs to be taken in our use of such material.

Raymond Brown articulated the difficulty, writing that the notion of prophecy as prediction of the distant future is no longer entertained by reputable Catholic and Protestant scholars.[44] He acknowledges that the New Testament's 'fulfilment' of the 'Old Testament' has involved much that the writers of the latter could never have foreseen. Prophets like Isaiah were concerned with addressing the circumstances prevailing when they lived. They knew nothing about 'Bethlehem' or 'Waco'.[45]

Brown makes these observations with regard to Greek Isaiah 7:14, but they have a wider application, especially to the Passion Narratives, and to the importance of contextualising biblical texts – that is, recognising the imperative for them to be interpreted in the totality of their circumstances. When, after the first century, later editors of the *LXX* corrected the mistranslation of Isaiah 7:14, they were honouring this principle.

Similarly, in 1952, when the editors of the *RSV* substituted 'young woman' for 'virgin' (Matthew 1:23) they were continuing the practice. Certain fundamentalist Christians, disapproving of the decision, purchased many copies of this Bible and proceeded to burn them.[46] (It should, however, be acknowledged that the United States' Conference of Catholic Bishops, against scholarly advice, imposed the reading 'virgin' instead of 'young woman' on their translators of the New American Bible.[47]) These fundamentalists are part of a long Christian tradition of book burning, and doubtless they would repudiate the closing paragraphs of this chapter.

It is seldom appreciated that at the time of Jesus virginity was understood in two ways, the usual one being virgo intacta (see Matthew 1:23). Genesis 24:16 provides an illustration: 'The girl was very beautiful, a virgin; no man had slept with her. Intercourse ends this type of virginity (parthenos).'[48] The second kind is where a girl is a virgin until she reaches puberty. Rabbinic Judaism's earliest law code, the Mishnah, defines a virgin as 'a girl who has never seen blood, even though she is married'.[49] This kind of virginity ends with menstruation.

Geza Vermes maintains that this is how Luke's Gospel understands the matter, because its account of the virginal conception is from a source other than Matthew's version, with no reference to Isaiah 7:14 (see Luke 1:26–35 and 2:5).[50]

The distinction is not a matter of academic hair-splitting. In a society that accepted child marriage, there was the possibility of a girl conceiving after her first ovulation but prior to her first period. In other words, she would be known as a virgin mother (mirabile dictu); writing c. 80 an eminent rabbi refers to a virgin mother bearing more than one child.[51] Vermes thus contends that Mary's reply to the angel – 'How can this be, since I am a virgin?' (1:34b) – should be rendered 'How can this be, for I have not yet begun to menstruate?'[52]

He argues further that nascent Christianity, by adopting two accounts of the virginal conception, turned away from the paradigm of legendary births attributed to iconic figures like Isaac, Jacob, Samuel and John the Baptist in favour of the 'totally novel belief in an act of divine impregnation, which belongs to the psychology of religion rather than to its history'.[53]

An obvious objection to Vermes's mirabile dictu hypothesis is that it is unnecessary. There are now two virginal conceptions, when actually we have none, reflecting an assessment by Sean Freyne (in a 1974 edition of The Furrow, a Catholic journal aimed at lay people) that Vermes's interpretation of Jesus the Jew is 'not stringent enough'.[54]

Vermes's point nonetheless is that the Infancy Narratives, late additions to Matthew and Luke, are instances of stories crafted in a milieu deeply influenced by Hellenistic thought. In The Changing Faces of Jesus, he argues that, by the end of the first century, 'Christianity had lost sight of Jesus and of his original message', which had found a home in 'alien surroundings'.[55] The Infancy Narratives are 'alien' to the real biography of Jesus, born in Nazareth, where he was most probably the first child of at least six others, two of whom were girls.[56]

Nowhere in the New Testament is the suggestion that these siblings were other than the natural children of Jesus' parents, and proposals to the contrary arise from a context long after Jesus' death and resurrection. There is irony here.

Many former Catholics have embraced various Protestant denominations because of official Catholicism's assertion about Mary Ever Virgin, which is a denial, as they perceive it, of the plain meaning of Mark 6:3, with its reference to Jesus' sisters and brothers. They have a point, but most of them then proceed to argue that the virginal conception of Jesus is 'historical fact', ignoring their own criterion of orthodoxy. Mark 6:3 does not make an exception of Jesus, for good reason: he was the natural child of Mary.[57]

They insist further that Christians who refuse to accept this litmus test of orthodoxy are not 'true believers', curiously embracing by a different route what they object to about Catholicism. No one should be denied the appellation 'Christian' on the basis of a refusal, for excellent theological and historical reasons, to interpret literally the virginal conception: no child's conception is open to biological investigation.[58]

Attempts to enforce this 'orthodoxy', which are becoming more strident in certain denominations, are misguided. The stories about the birth of Jesus can support later doctrinal teachings (that Jesus is God and that Mary was conceived 'immaculately', for instance) only in a tangential, not a literal, sense. These accounts, of themselves, do not validate such doctrines, and it is disingenuous to claim otherwise, given what we now know about their midrashic origins.

It is impossible to understand the birth narratives without recognising their Jewish background as midrashic creations and, for those who wish to interpret these stories as accounts of events in real time, they need to provide an interpretation of them without recourse to one that violates Raymond Brown's caution that 'Christianity can never seek refuge in anything but the truth'.[59]

How, then, should we understand the Infancy Narratives?

CHAPTER 4

Heroes of Divine Origin

*The Star of Bethlehem and
obliteration of the Earth*

One interpretation is that the Infancy Narratives reflect 'conventional Hellenistic biographies of famous persons'. These figures were often said to have had at least one divinity as a parent (Mithras, for example).[60] The evangelists accounted for Jesus' life and noble death in terms that enhanced his comparison with the lives of these heroic and portentous characters.

Aristoxenus (d. 310 BCE) was a student of Aristotle. His biography, typical of accounts of the lives of such people, comprises five key elements:

- ▶ an unusual birth
- ▶ revealing childhood episodes
- ▶ wise teachings
- ▶ accounts of wondrous deeds
- ▶ the 'achievement' of a noble death (Socrates' death, after that of Jesus, is the most famous one in the ancient world)

The Gospels of Matthew and Luke mirror these elements, and thus are 'examples of Hellenistic biography'.[61]

Lane McGaughey has undertaken an extensive study of infancy narratives in the ancient world, identifying six characteristics shared by all of them:

1. genealogies of illustrious ancestors
2. unusual (miraculous) conceptions/births
3. dream encounters and/or accompanying angelic announcements
4. praise for the birth and the forecast of great things to come
5. births with accompanying supernatural portents
6. the hostile response of competitors/persecutors to the hero's birth[62]

The parallels with the Infancy Narratives are clear. Matthew, for example, provides an extensive genealogy going back to Abraham (1:1–17) and Luke's genealogy extends back to Adam (3:23–38). Their intention is not to furnish historical information.

1   These 'genealogies' convey the meaning that Jesus is believed to have fulfilled a particular destiny, not authenticate a 'birth certificate'; in the same way, 'Bethlehem' does not identify his place of origin.

'Abraham', who is a symbol of Jewish identity and piety, is thus seen to endorse the messianic status attributed to Jesus. The role of 'Adam' is to represent the affirmation that Jesus has inaugurated a mission of universal significance. It is extremely unlikely in that Jesus was aware of, let alone endorsed, such claims.

2
The criterion of 'unusual conceptions' speaks for itself. (That of John the Baptist applies in this context, since it is a *lesser* miracle preparatory to the revelation of a *greater* miracle; see Luke 1:5-24 and point 4, below – 'Elizabeth' *is* 'Hannah').

3
'Dream Encounters' figure prominently in Matthew's Infancy Gospel, where there are five: one of them is an experience of the 'Wise Men', and the remaining four pertain to St Joseph: 'Get, up, take the child and his mother and go to the land of Israel, for those who were seeking the child's life are dead' (2:20), for example.

Luke's Gospel has none, though there may be an allusion to a dream when it was revealed to Simeon that 'he would not see death before he had seen the Lord's Messiah' (2:26).

4
'Praise and Forecast' are clearly evident in Luke's narration of Jesus' Presentation in the Temple (2:22-38), a midrash on the story of Hannah and Elkanah in 1 Samuel 1-2, where Samuel, child of the barren Hannah, is presented to the Lord (1:27-28). Simeon praises God, taking the baby Jesus in his arms and declaring that the child is 'destined for the falling and rising of many in Israel', predicting that a sword will pierce Mary's heart (2:33-35).

Part of the background to the Presentation is that it reflects Judaism's repudiation of an earlier pagan practice where the family's firstborn son was sacrificed to the tribal god, the meaning behind sacrificing the 'turtle-doves and pigeons' (Luke 2:24b).[63]

Anna, also present in the Temple, praises God, forecasting that Jesus will realise 'the redemption of Jerusalem' (Luke 2:36-38).

These excerpts indicate that the Birth Narratives were composed after the Passion Narratives, demonstrated particularly by reference to the 'piercing sword' (a likely midrash on Ezekiel 14:17).

The hero's fate in these ancient birth narratives was always in some manner known or predetermined, to be understood ultimately in the light of his noble end, reflecting Kierkegaard's famous precept quoted in Chapter 2.

5 The two 'Supernatural Portents' are the Heavenly Host (Luke) and the Star (Matthew), what Hubert Richards calls the 'tinselly bits'.

Most years, in December, 'learned scientific articles' are produced about the Star of Bethlehem, and in 2017 *The Irish Times* did not fail its readership. A retired UCD professor of mathematics speculated that the star may be accounted for by known astrological phenomena at the time, including the appearance of Halley's Comet. He neglected to inform the newspaper's eager readers that, for a stopping star to behave in the manner described in Matthew 2:9, it would have caused the Earth's obliteration.[64] The good professor needs a short course in midrash. It is also noteworthy that the apocryphal Proto-Gospel of James relates the claim that 'time stood still' when Jesus was born (18:2).

6 The 'Persecution theme' is present in Herod's Massacre of the Innocents (see Chapter 6).

Two interesting features of ancient birth narratives are that, if the hero is a human being, the miracle is that a barren woman conceives (Isaac and John the Baptist, for instance), and, if superhuman, the male parent is a god.[65] Examples of the latter type are Hercules and Alexander the Great (d. 323 BCE).

Plato (d. 348 BCE), the West's most influential philosopher, is also illustrative of this phenomenon.[66] Legend has it that Ariston, Plato's father, stopped making love to his wife Perictone, because she was unable to conceive. Apollo, Greek god of archery, music, prophecy and of the sun, then appeared in a dream to Ariston to inform him of Plato's imminent birth, which occurred on Apollo's birthday, the implication being that he is Plato's 'father'. Plato is thus said to be human and divine.[67]

The point of the legend, related by an author in the third century of our era, is this: 'How could Plato, a mere mortal, have produced writings of such genius, without himself being somehow immortal, like a god?' Of interest also is an ode written in Plato's honour where, like Elijah, he is translated into the celestial realms.[68]

These stories are said to complement the view that, by c. 80, the evangelists were beginning to push back claims about Jesus' messianic status to his birth and reinforcing them by asserting that his unusual life and death mirrored the lives and deaths of other famous people: 'Each of their noble lives, according to reports, had been preceded by an unusual birth and infancy, so Jesus' birth and life must also have been portentous.'[69]

The Infancy Narratives came to serve an additional purpose. Christians, influenced by the Christological doctrines of Nicaea and Chalcedon, so emphasise the 'uniqueness' of Jesus that we forget the philosophical and religious heritage of the Mediterranean world that contributed to, if it did not entirely create, the Birth Stories about him.

A tragic consequence of this development is that, whatever their original intention, the Infancy Narratives soon produced a situation whereby theological speculation about Jesus lost touch with his Jewish origins. This made Jesus an 'easy sell' to Gentiles, culminating in the (heretical) teachings of Marcion (d. 160), one of the more intriguing and provocative figures of primitive Christianity. He rejected the God of Judaism.[70]

In time, that 'easy sell', and the succeeding centuries of vilification directed at Jews led by a circuitous route, via the racial anti-Semitism of the nineteenth century, to the Holocaust. This Teaching of Vilification (Contempt) was the necessary, but not the sufficient, cause of that great catastrophe.

Raymond Brown acknowledges that Graeco-Roman modes of thinking would have been available to Jewish-Christians in Palestine and the Diaspora, but he disputes the claim that the Infancy Narratives make sense exclusively within the world of Hellenism.

He observes that pagan legends of the births of famous people 'often involved gross or amoral sexual conduct on the part of the deity who was thought to have begotten the child'.[71] Romans 1:24 suggests how Jewish-Christians would have understood these scenarios: 'God gave them up in the lusts of their hearts to impurity, to the degrading of their bodies among themselves.' Brown notes also that, in the first century, when Christians compared the virginal conception story with pagan birth legends, 'they could see no affinity but rather a sharp contrast between the two'.[72]

He maintains further that none of these divinely engendered births parallel the non-sexual virginal conception of Jesus, arguing 'there is no clear example of virginal conception in world or pagan religions that could have given first-century Jewish-Christians this idea.'[73]

These objections fail to convince, for the reason that we are dealing with the adaptation of an idea, not a slavish imitation of lascivious Graeco-Roman mythology.

Furthermore, Luke's reference to the power of the Most High overshadowing Mary, preceded by citing the Holy Spirit as enabler of the conception (1:35), is ambivalent, to say the least. He, contrary to the 'spin' of providing his readers with 'an orderly account of the events that have been fulfilled among us' and handed on by eyewitnesses (1:1-2), was really giving us a lesson in theology, not obstetrics, and he knew it.

Justin Martyr (d. 165), in his Dialogue with Trypho the Jew, used Greek Isaiah 7:14 as a 'proof text' for the claim about Jesus' conception (see Matthew 1:23). Rabbi Trypho made a surprisingly modern objection to Justin, when he said that the verse had been cited out of its historical context, continuing with the observation that Matthew 1:23 is explicable only with reference to Greek mythology, recounting the story of Perseus, who was allegedly begotten of Danae, a virgin.[74]

Trypho (he may be a literary creation, like Barabbas), at the risk of labouring the point, insists that the idea of a conceiving parthenos is entirely contrary to the intention of Hebrew Isaiah 7:14, the source of the Greek translation, which in turn created a mythological account of Jesus' birth as the fulfilment of prophecy.

One consequence of Justin's Dialogue is that it contributed to the process whereby Christianity effectively appropriated the Hebrew Bible for its own ends. This observation needs to be contextualised by noting that the original Jewish-Christians ('Messianic Jews') did not consider themselves to be looters of the traditions they accessed from the Hebrew Bible: rabbinic Judaism and primitive Christianity 'arose with equal validity and complete integrity from the common matrix of Second Temple Judaism'.[75]

However, the purpose of the Dialogue, written much later, is to demonstrate both that Gentile Christianity replaces

Judaism and that the 'Logos' of Greek philosophy is really the God of the 'Old Testament'. (Justin believed that Christianity fulfilled all that was best in philosophy, especially Platonism.) Christians, by the middle of the second century, thus ignored legitimate objections to the manner in which the Jewish Scriptures were being interpreted in a Gentile milieu alien to their original context and purpose.

These observations alert us also to the consideration that Justin Martyr would not have concocted this series of debates had they not reflected major controversies at the time, centred particularly on the fact that Jesus does not fulfil messianic expectations.[76]

Justin, like many Christians today, failed to ask the right questions of the Infancy Narratives, just as in the past there was the mistaken expectation that the Book of Genesis provided factual historical and scientific information. The writers of these narratives, to paraphrase Hubert Richards, never intended them to be understood as biological and historical accounts of Jesus' birth, and to defend their historicity against all comers is to invite people to reject the perennial religious insights they contain.[77]

He makes the further point that the 'tinselly bits' of the Christmas Story – the angels, the star and the celestial choir, for example – have 'the magic power to take us out of our mean selves', but if all they succeed in doing is banishing Jesus to 'an unreal world of fairy-lights', then we are better off without them.[78]

This chapter provides some insights into the provenance of the Infancy Narratives, but it is far from being the whole story. The fuller picture requires a continuing appreciation of the role of midrash in shaping these stories, beginning with the Three Wise Men. In approaching their story, we need to ask the right questions about it, as we do with all literature, ancient and modern. The famous account of 'gold, frankincense and myrrh' invites the question, 'What does it mean?', not 'Did it happen?'

CHAPTER 5

The Queen of Sheba Visits Bethlehem

*The Roman Birthday of the Sun
became the Christian Birthday
of the Son.*

In Cologne Cathedral, situated above the high altar, there is a magnificent shrine traditionally believed to have contained the bones of the Three Kings. Their 'remains' were originally interred in Constantinople and brought to Cologne, via Milan, by Frederick Barbarossa, Holy Roman Emperor (d. 1190). The cathedral was built to house the shrine and in 1864 it was discovered to contain the bones of Philip I (d. 1191), Archbishop of Cologne.

The shrine's fascinating history is a metaphor for the even more unusual origins of St Matthew's account of the Three Wise Men who allegedly visited the baby Jesus. His gospel tells us that, in the time of Herod, 'Wise men from the East came to Jerusalem' (2:1). This is one of Matthew's ways of articulating how Jesus' followers, having experienced the Easter Moment, set about interpreting it by discovering the promise(s) that foretold it, fulfilling a purpose similar to that of Simeon's prophecy about the baby Jesus, recounted in the previous chapter.

Midrash, derived from the Hebrew verb darash, means 'to search out', with the connotation of going in pursuit of something awaiting discovery. And that is precisely what the Wise Men do. They pursue a wandering star to Bethlehem, having been told by Herod to 'search diligently for the child' (2:8).

Matthew derived much of the story from the Book of Numbers. There, Balaam, a Gentile prophet from the East, has been hired by Balak to damn Israel: 'Come now, curse this people for me' (22:6). Instead, Balaam pronounces a blessing: 'A star shall come out of Jacob, and a sceptre shall rise out of Israel' (24:17b), and this is where the Star of Bethlehem comes from – all the UCD mathematics professor had to do was read the Book of Numbers.

The significance of this story, like that of the census, is the claim that Jesus, not Caesar, is now the figure of universal significance. Our professor was concerned to convey to the readers of *The Irish Times* how the star worked, but his worthy efforts entirely miss the point. The story of the star – and those of the angelic chorus and shepherds keeping watch over their flock for that matter – was not told to make 'children goggle in amazement'. These stories are really 'parables', told to exemplify claims being made c. 80 about Jesus, representing a theological meditation on that originating Easter Moment.[79]

There is no requirement to take literally the warning to the Wise Men in a dream 'not to return to Herod' (2:12), no more than is it necessary to ascribe a factual basis to the angel's appearance to Joseph, telling him to take Mary and the child to Egypt because Herod wanted to kill him (2:13). We should understand the angelic announcements of the Infancy Narratives as mirroring those of the Resurrection Narratives:

> After the Sabbath, as the first day of the week was dawning, Mary Magdalene and the other Mary went to see the tomb. And suddenly there was a great earthquake; for an angel of the Lord, descending from Heaven, came and rolled back the stone and sat on it. (Matthew 28:1–2)

In other words, the accounts of Jesus' death and resurrection were composed before the Infancy Gospels were written. It is mistaken to think that Herod's supposed attempt to murder Jesus, for example, anticipated in real time his death some thirty years later. The truth is the other way round. Jesus' death and resurrection took place first, before Matthew and Luke wrote their Birth Stories. Their narratives 'are an echo of that event, not a foretaste of it'.[80]

It is no accident that the (canonical) Resurrection Narratives reflect the motif of 'light'. St Mark, the earliest writer, relates that the sun had just risen when the women arrived at the tomb (16:2). The sun illuminated the reality of Jesus' resurrection, just as the Star of Bethlehem illuminated his birth. In later Jewish folklore, stars were said to have announced the births of Abraham, Isaac and Moses, and another legend has it that the parents of Moses were said to have been made aware in advance of their son's auspicious identity.

Our galaxy, known popularly as the Milky Way, has more than 200 billion stars, and most of them are larger and emanate more light than our life-giving star, the sun.[81] It is little wonder that 'light' is an ancient and powerfully evocative symbol. Starlight announced portentous events on Earth, 'in a world that viewed the sky as the roof of the Earth and the floor of Heaven'.[82]

The Hebrew Bible provides many examples of 'light', and probably the most famous one is from Isaiah, known to millions of people courtesy of Handel's famous oratorio, *Messiah*: 'The people who walked in darkness have seen a great light; those who lived in darkness ... , on them light has shined' (Isaiah 9:2). Isaiah continues by referencing that 'a child has been born for us', and he is named 'Wonderful Counsellor, Mighty God, Everlasting Father, Prince of Peace' (Isaiah 9:6), which is how Handel orchestrated Isaiah's light motif.

We take light for granted in a world lit up by electricity, but the majority of the world's population could not afford candles until c. 1800. Our ancestors experienced darkness in a way that we do not.[83] It is against this background that we should in part understand Simeon's proclamation of Jesus as 'a light of revelation to the Gentiles', but serving primarily a metaphorical purpose (Luke 2:32a).

Luke's Gospel was almost certainly written at Antioch (the empire's third-largest city), for Gentile Christians living there. But these 'Syrian Christians' never celebrated Christmas as we do, for the reason that nobody knew then (nor do we know now), the year, season, month or day of Jesus' birth. The imperative to record biographical data is a modern one.[84]

It was Pope Julius I (d. 352) who decided that 25 December should be 'Christmas Day', prior to which the birth of Jesus had been celebrated at various times between March and November, thereby supplanting the Winter Solstice Festival dedicated to the Birthday of the Unconquered Sun (Mithras, in effect).[85] Julius switched the Birthday of the Sun for the Birthday of the Son, , note Borg and Crossan, an amazing 'spin exercise' in what today would be described as a brilliant marketing coup. 'Night' became 'Light'.

The symbolism is present in the first line of the beautiful Christmas carol: 'Silent night, holy night, all is calm, all is bright'.[86] It is represented also by The Star of Bethlehem, which is the radiance that draws the (Gentile) Wise Men into the orbit of Simeon's 'light of revelation to the Gentiles' (Luke 2:32).

Christian tradition has typically referred to the Wise Men as the Three Kings, epitomised by their 'resting place' in Cologne Cathedral. Historical theology provides a better interpretation. The Wise Men, like Judas in the Passion Stories, are characters in a parabolic narrative, no more historical than the Arthurian legend of Camelot.

Raymond Brown has noted that, in Jewish legends of the period, the pharaoh was the recipient of counsel given by wise elders (Magi).[87] The visit of the Magi, from which we get the word 'magician', is Matthew's way of saying that 'Gentiles from the East' acknowledged that the 'King of the Jews' is also their king.[88] We have three kings because Matthew tells us they brought three gifts to Bethlehem: gold, frankincense and myrrh (Matthew 2:11b).

He sourced this midrash not from Numbers, but from Isaiah 60: 'Nations shall come to your light and kings to the brightness of your dawn ... They shall bring gold and frankincense, praising the Lord' (vv. 3 to 6).[89] 'Myrrh' is omitted from this account, but its presence in Matthew's narrative probably derives from 1 Kings 10:1–13, where the Queen of Sheba pays a visit to Solomon, 'with camels bearing spices and gold' (v.2).

Psalm 72:10 refers to the 'Kings of Tarshish and Sheba', and to 'gifts', which provided an additional source for Matthew, and Geza Vermes has remarked that the visit of the Armenian King Tiradetes to worship the Emperor-god Nero, may have prompted the introduction of the Magi into the narrative. Pliny the Elder says that Tiradetes' courtiers were known as 'Magi'.[90]

When all of these considerations are taken together, we can recognise the Queen of Sheba's symbolic pilgrimage to worship the Babe of Bethlehem. Luke situates it at the time 'while Quirinius was governor of Syria, following a decree from Augustus 'that all the world should be registered' (Luke 2:1–2). An enormous quantity of academic ink has been spilt discussing Quirinius' Census.

If the premise of this book is right, that the Infancy Narratives, with two exceptions pertaining to Herod the Great and Archelaus, provide us with no historical data, the puzzle is solved. As with the Magi, we are dealing with symbolism, not history.

Marcus Borg and Dominic Crossan explain this parabolic census and its subsequent implications when they write that 'Roman imperial theology and early Christian theology both assert the same titles for Jesus: Divine, Son of God, Lord, Redeemer, God from God and Saviour of the World'.[91] The point is not whether there was a census in the probable year of Jesus' birth (there was not), but that the claim invites people to make a choice, between the 'divine Augustus', who employed a policy of peace through violence, and Jesus, who embraced a vision of peace through justice.[92]

It is likely, however, that Luke has adapted midrashically the first Roman census of Palestine in 6 CE to suit his theological vision, particularly in light of the fact that he must surely have known that it was not Roman practice to apply such measures throughout the empire. Governors made local arrangements for taxation purposes.

On the other hand, there is the remote possibility that, in the last year of his life, Herod the Great conducted his own census and Luke has confused this with the one of 6 CE. An Egyptian papyrus from 104 CE includes an ordinance for such a census, and it is noteworthy that women had to be present.[93] In Palestine, however, it was the head of household only that had responsibility for completing the registration, and in any case Joseph, on the assumption that he is not a narrative device, would have undertaken this duty in Galilee, not in Bethlehem to the south, had there indeed been a census.

Furthermore, we know that the Romans exempted their 'allied kings', a term used by Geza Vermes in his last book – The True Herod, published posthumously – from such interference from the central government at Rome.[94]

What also supports the argument against historicity for a Roman census in 4 BCE, in addition to the consideration that Jesus' birth that year would have meant he was ten or eleven years old when Quirinius' census was conducted, is that ancient history has no example of requiring people to return to the ancestral home for the purpose of registration pertaining to tax or any other matter.[95]

In addition, Luke 2:1–5 presupposes a level of governmental efficiency and record-keeping that does not exist today, let alone more than 2,000 years ago, in a world without birth, marriage and death certificates.[96]

It was also a society whose modes of transportation were primitive. It is about 135 kilometres from Nazareth to Bethlehem, a journey of between seven and ten days on a donkey, with no 'restaurant services' en route. No sensible husband would subject his heavily pregnant wife to that ordeal.[97]

What clinches the fact that we are dealing with symbolism, not history, is this gospel's genealogy (3:23–38), which is inevitably conflated with Luke's account of the census, for understandable reasons. The genealogy has forty-one generations between David and Joseph. The number of direct descendants in that time (of a notional 1,000 years) would have been in the millions, leaving to one side the added consideration that King David had many wives.[98]

The idea that any government would know these 'millions' and King David's 'heirs', ordering them back to Bethlehem, is preposterous, if read literally. No city in the ancient world could have accommodated that influx of people. Indeed, no metropolis in the modern world is capable of such an 'accommodation'.[99] There would, quite literally, have been 'no room at the inn' (Luke 2:7b).

Robert Karris OFM remarks that the 'inn' and 'manger' perform symbolic functions. Jesus is placed in the latter wearing 'swaddling clothes', clearly alluding to Solomon, Jesus' predecessor on the throne of David: 'I was nursed with care in swaddling clothes' (Wisdom 7:4).[100] The pathos-evoking 'No room at the inn' actually represents the beautiful idea that 'Jesus is the one who will be host to starving humanity', and the manger therein (referenced three times) reinforces this idea, because it represents symbolically a significant theme of this gospel – that of food.[101]

Luke cleverly suggests that Jesus, despite having been born in 'lowly circumstances', is he who can address all of humanity's material and spiritual needs, a theme 'resurrected' when the adult Jesus, as the Servant about to lay down his life, hosts a meal in a guest-room that his disciples will continue to commemorate in his memory (see 22: 10-13 and the Institution of the Eucharist, 22: 14-23).[102]

The census is simply Luke's brilliant literary-historical device for getting Mary and Joseph to Bethlehem, in order to fulfil Davidic expectation. Shakespeare, had he been writing plays in our century, would have applauded the device, of which he made extensive use.

At Lent and Advent, Christians are invited to address this question: 'Do we think that peace on Earth can be realised through 'Caesar' or 'Christ'?' Luke's answer is Jesus, symbolised by his tender story of shepherds tending their flocks (2:8). They symbolise people everywhere who are marginalised by political and religious systems.[103] In addition, the shepherds theme is a deliberate echo of King David's humble origins as a shepherd (see 1 Samuel 16:1-13). In other words, it is a midrash.[104]

CHAPTER 6

—

Better to be Herod's Pig than Herod's Son

'Down with the Jews, they kill innocent children!'

NORWICH, ENGLAND
1144 AND LIMERICK, IRELAND, 1904/5

'Humility' was not in the repertoire of Herod the Great's personality traits. By any standards, he was a homicidal maniac, but the one 'crime' he did not commit is the mythical Massacre of the Innocents (Matthew 2:16–18).

The term 'myth' has frequently been employed by academics in their study of the Infancy Narratives, which lies partly behind Chapter 4's 'Divine Heroes', but if 'myth' signifies fictions that cannot be taken seriously it fails to communicate the richness of the concept, leading to superficial judgements about religious narratives.[105]

Myth, properly experienced, is a source of spiritual transformation, and unless an event like Jesus' birth, with all the mythical trappings surrounding it – the angelic chorus and the story of the murder of toddlers, for instance – cannot be liberated from the confines of a specific time and place, and brought into the life of Christians living in a world after Copernicus and Darwin, it will deservedly perish.[106]

The purpose of myth is not to provide information. It is to invite people to embrace truths that are as invisible as music yet as positive as sound, to paraphrase Emily Dickinson in a very different context.

When, every year, we pray before nativity scenes, believers are participating in a powerful ritual reflecting the positive sounds of that first and *invisible* Silent Night. Christians know the Christmas story to be true, not because it conforms to a checklist of historical data but because of its power to transform lives.

We impoverish the wonder of religion when it is reduced to 'argument' and 'theology'. Arguments, no matter how erudite, seldom change people. Only stories, not legend or dogma, have the power to address 'the better angels of our nature', as Jesus and Abraham Lincoln knew so well, because they give us the hope of a future redeemed from the terrors of the past.

Religious mythology is not to be identified with legends or fairy tales, which are clearly not factual, but they typically serve a didactic purpose. Myth and story, however, availing of the analogical and oblique nature of religious language, communicate truths of enduring significance.

One medieval legend, with a definite purpose obliquely reflecting the myth-midrash of Herod's Murder of the Innocents, comes from the Tyrol in modern Austria. It tells of 'little Catholic children being kidnapped by Jews so that they could be murdered in one of the services held in the synagogue'.[107]

The legend is typical of many circulating at the time, the most infamous one concerning William of Norwich, who was twelve years old when he disappeared a few days after Easter 1144. He was known to the city's Jewish community. His slain and mutilated body was found by a nun and a forester.[108] Thomas of Monmouth, a Benedictine monk, writing ten years later, produced 'evidence' that 'the Jews abducted William for demonic ritual purposes, subjecting him to the cruellest of tortures and a slow, agonizing death'.[109] His mother, according to Thomas, unwittingly gave the child to 'a Jew', for which she was paid three (silver) shillings, a clear allusion to Judas's supposed betrayal of Jesus for thirty pieces of silver (DJJ argues that Judas did not betray Jesus, and that the claim is a midrash on 1 Corinthians 11:23–24).

Thomas' legendary account of William's murder presents him as a Christian martyr who worked miracles, and 'the key to appreciating his death lay in the murderous guilt of the Jews', who 'scourged and crucified William, just as the Jews of Judaea had scourged and crucified Jesus'.[110]

'Blood' is a theme common to these grotesque fantasies, where the purpose of 'demonic rituals' is to extract and drink children's blood, clearly parodying the Last Supper. Thomas argued further that one of the reasons why the Jews targeted William was because his innocence made him more susceptible to their 'financial avarice'.

Most historians agree that the Norwich ritual murder libel of 1144 was 'the first of its kind in Medieval Europe', providing a template for 'many similar accusations that would come in its wake'.[111]

Early in the thirteenth century an Austrian poet wrote:

> In every year it happens still
> The Jews Christ's Passion offer,
> When a Christian boy they kill.[112]

The *Catholic Encyclopaedia* renounces the preposterous claims of ritual murder, but it then proceeds with the extraordinary observation that Jews may have murdered 'some of these victims' because of their odium fidei, that is, Jewish hatred of Christianity.[113] What 'victims'? There were no child victims of ritual murder, but countless Jews have been murdered by hateful Christians.

The legend almost certainly had a long oral tradition prior to its literary representations in the twelfth century, which soon spread throughout Europe, and that oral tradition is related to a misunderstanding of the story about King Herod killing 'the children in and around Bethlehem who were two years old or younger' (Matthew 2:16).

Ireland has been almost entirely free of overt anti-Semitism, with one major exception: The Limerick Boycott of 1904/5. One night in January 1904, a large mob converged on the homes and businesses of the small number of Jews residing in Limerick.[114] The mob had come directly from a gathering of the Archconfraternity of the Holy Family, at which, supported by referencing libels and slanders of ritual murder, and naming so-called 'martyr victims' ('William' probably had a mention), a sermon had been given by a Redemptorist priest, John Creagh, in which he asserted:

- ▶ that the Jews, because of their 'financial avarice', were responsible for enslaving the people of Limerick to usury;

- that they murdered *the Christ*;
- that the citizens of Limerick must immediately boycott Jewish businesses.

A week later, Creagh (d. 1947) repeated the same allegations, this time exhorting the confraternity members not to resort to violence.[115] Early the following year, a reporter from The Jewish Chronicle visited Limerick, where he witnessed Jews being attacked 'right and left', with some having to run for their lives. He reported organised protests, with the mob yelling 'Down with the Jews, they kill innocent children.'[116]

Creagh exploited and inflamed the consequences of the Dreyfus Affair (1894–99) and the appalling Kishinev Pogrom of 1903 in Russia, which occasioned a massive surge to the West of Eastern European Jews. It is a mercy that, unlike at Kishinev, there were no fatalities in Limerick.

These crimes were fuelled by the rise of late nineteenth-century racial anti-Semitism and Creagh had tapped into a religious and historical sewer, reflecting the opprobrious Teaching of Contempt, typified by Thomas of Monmouth's lies. The William Legend that had originated in twelfth-century Norwich erupted again in twentieth-century Limerick, and probably had its remote origins in a first-century midrash about Jesus as the 'new Moses', written about eighty years after Herod's death.

Herod the Great was recognised by Rome as 'King of the Jews' in 40 BCE, gaining full control of his territories three years later (37). 'Herod' means 'sprung from a hero'.[117] There is little doubt that history does not judge Herod to be heroic. Of his many children, Herod certainly murdered three of them and possibly more, in addition to having his favourite wife of ten, Mariamne, strangled. For good measure, Herod also executed Alexandra (his mother-in-law), her brother and Mariamne's grandfather and brother, and countless others (garrotting and burning to death were the preferred means of dispatching his victims).

Pigs, however, were safe from Herod's murderous reach, as demonstrated by Caesar Augustus' sardonic quip, 'Better to be Herod's pig than Herod's son', knowing that Herod – a Jew – would abstain from pork.[118]

It is little wonder that people have no difficulty believing Herod to have murdered children, but he is entirely innocent of the 'crime'. There was no Massacre of the Innocents. The purpose of the story is to draw a parallel between Pharaoh's (probably unhistorical) efforts to kill the infant Moses and Jesus as the 'new Moses', who will ultimately meet a violent end. It has nothing to do with the Herod of history, who is deservedly famed for his extensive building programme, in particular the extension to the Temple – probably the most resplendent building of the ancient world.

Matthew has constructed the story as a parallelism between Moses the Great and Jesus the Greater, illustrated also by their manner of escape: for Moses, it is away from Egypt; for Jesus it is into Egypt.[119] In other words, the place of past oppression and despair for Moses becomes a centre of hope and refuge for Jesus.[120]

This hope motif is intended for Matthew's readers, and he communicates it employing a brilliant narrative device when the Magi reach Jerusalem, having them ask, 'Where is the child who has been born King of the Jews?' (2:2b). Herod then inquires of his advisers where the Messiah is to be born (2:4), and in this context 'Messiah' is a synonym for 'King of the Jews'. This second title is not employed again until the Passion Narratives, where it figures three times, typically when Pilate asks, 'Are you the King of the Jews?' (27:11).[121]

The background is the year 40 BCE when Mark Antony and Octavian contrived to make Herod 'King of the Jews', and its use in this Infancy Narrative is intended as an overture to the gospel, culminating on Calvary, when the inscription 'King of the Jews' is placed at the head of the cross (27:37). Its role as the gospel's bookend is a reminder that the objective of the Roman-appointed Herod who sought to kill Jesus was finally achieved by another Roman, Pilate.[122]

Matthew is telling us that the shadow of Roman imperial dominance, present at Jesus' birth, would not be allowed to triumph by his death, which explains the words attributed to the (Gentile) centurion at the foot of the cross, 'Truly, this man was God's son' (27:54).[123]

Whoever wrote Matthew's Gospel would also have made a superb thriller writer, dropping brilliant indicators like bookends, headers and footers into the plot.

The Massacre of the Innocents and almost all of the material in the Passion Narratives are not recorded history, but rather exercises in retrospective theology, and this is also how we should understand Rachel's voice raised in Ramah, wailing and weeping for her children (2:18). It is used as a fulfilment citation, from Jeremiah 31:15, to indicate that Herod's putative slaughter of children was fore-ordained, but it has additional symbolic importance.

Ramah is where 600 years earlier the Babylonians had kept their Jewish captives prior to deportation to Mesopotamia (587/6). Matthew's purpose is to establish a midrashic association between the two occurrences, the point being that Jesus' temporary exile in Egypt will eventually result in a better outcome for his people than the disaster occasioned by the Babylonian Exile (of course, Matthew had no way of knowing that, 2,000 years later, millions of Jesus' people would perish in the Holocaust).[124]

The Babylonian Exile came to an end in 539 BCE, when Cyrus, King of Persia, permitted the Jews to return to their homeland.[125] (Of interest is the likelihood that the exiles brought back with them, derived from Zoroastrianism, beliefs about resurrection from the dead.)

Another fulfilment citation is the one that attests to the Flight into Egypt: 'Out of Egypt, I have called my son' (Hosea 11:1). Raymond Brown observes that the verse referred originally to the Exodus from Egypt, and Matthew interpreted it in relation to Jesus, 'who relives in his own life the history of that people'.[126] Geza Vermes notes that the Flight into Egypt presents us with an Exodus in reverse, providing the circumstances whereby Jesus can return to Israel, in fulfilment of the Hosea citation.[127]

As with 'prophecy', there is a problem with 'fulfilment citations'. The difficulty is that they are presented in terms of Jesus alone being able to fulfil them, typified by the misattribution of Greek Isaiah 7:14, discussed earlier.

Matthew and other New Testament writers employ this methodology, which in essentials is an exercise in midrashic selectivism, critiqued by Paula Fredriksen:

> ▸ Matthew in particular is engaged in an exercise of 'theological appropriation', meaning that his use of citation/proof-texts suggest implicitly 'the incompletion of Judaism', which soon thereafter led to the popular 'Christian' belief that Jesus had abrogated his ancestral faith – nothing could be further from the historical truth.

- ▶ This Gospel has chosen selected quotations, chiefly from Isaiah, Jeremiah and the Minor Prophets (Micah, for instance). They are notoriously ambiguous and replete with metaphors.
- ▶ The remainder of the Hebrew Bible, however, does not lend itself so easily to such interpretations, the consequence being that all of Scripture's teachings become focused on *Jesus the Christ* and only those texts considered to support this 'identification' are deemed of relevance.[128]

Fredriksen's observations matter because they highlight a problem that besets Christianity to this day – its implicit and sometimes explicit assumption that first-century Judaism rejected Jesus as the 'Promised One'. It did no such thing, for a variety of reasons, and not least because the historical Jesus almost certainly made no such claim on his own behalf, no more than Judaism when he was alive subscribed to belief in a divine Messianic figure.

Jesus died a loyal son of the covenant and it is therefore wholly inappropriate to accuse Jews of a failure to recognise 'their Messiah', an accusation that has had disastrous consequences for the ancestors of Jesus the Jew, culminating in the abomination that is the Holocaust.

By the early second century, however, when emerging (Gentile) Christianity began to interpret literally Herod's Massacre of the Innocents, it had unwittingly cast the die for a developing hostile relationship between Judaism and Christianity, typified by some of the Apocryphal gospels, including those pertaining to Jesus' childhood:

When a Jew saw what Jesus had done, while playing with friends at a stream, he went to Joseph and complained that his son, having turned soft clay into twelve sparrows, had profaned the Sabbath.[129]

CHAPTER 7

A Problem Child

*He saddled the donkey and seated
her on it; and his son led it along,
while Joseph followed behind.*

The late Rabbi Lionel Blue (d. 2016) told me a great story about Franco Zeffirelli's film-series *Jesus of Nazareth*, starring Robert Powell. It has a coming-of-age scene in which the boy Jesus, aged twelve, celebrates his bar mitzvah ('confirmation' in Christianity).

Zeffirelli had clearly read Luke's account of the boy Jesus in the Temple (2:41–52), and for understandable but mistaken reasons he deduced that this was a practice common in the first century, presumably mirroring the director's own experience when a Catholic adolescent. (It is not unusual to hear Christian homilists interpret the passage in a similar manner.) He had neglected, however, to research the background to bar mitzvah. As a Jewish practice, there is no evidence of this ceremony prior to the fifteenth century.

Much of the movie was filmed in Tunisia and a local played the role of the boy Jesus, who – as 'tradition' decreed – read from the Torah (in phonetic Hebrew) as part of the ceremony. Despite countless retakes, the boy kept stumbling over the words. At this juncture, one of Zeffirelli's assistants suggested that Blue might be able to help with the 'problem child', and he was flown to Tunisia. Much to Zeffirelli's annoyance, Blue had no more success in tutoring the boy than had a previous local rabbi. Exasperated, he said, 'Franco, every little Jewish boy "stumbles" through his bar mitzvah and, in any case, there was no such ceremony when Jesus was alive', to which the great director replied: 'Lionel, every little Jewish boy may stumble through his bar mitzvah, but not the Son of God!'

This charming story of how Zeffirelli insisted that audiences expected to see a bar mitzvah in the movie illustrates how religious practices and beliefs seldom conform to some idealised notion of historical truth, an observation that applies also to the place of the Virgin Mary in Christian tradition.

Luke has Mary reprimand another problem youngster: 'Child, why have you treated us like this?' (2:48b), after three days of looking for Jesus. 'Your father and I have been searching for you with great anxiety' (2:49).

He replies: 'I must be in my Father's house' (2:50b). We are then told that Jesus returned with them to Nazareth, increasing in wisdom, and that divine and human favour was upon him (2:52).

We easily miss two significant implications of these verses:

- ▶ The 'three days' reference is theological, not chronological. It is a motif that first appears in its written form when Abraham is commanded to sacrifice Isaac, his son (Genesis 22, see v.4, with pagan resemblances). It is most famously associated by no accident with Jesus' resurrection (Mark 16:2 and

- When v.52 refers to 'increasing in wisdom' it clearly reflects one of the characteristics attributed to heroes of the ancient world (see Aristoxenus, Chapter 4).

Robert Karris OFM observes that a curious feature of the story of the boy Jesus in the Temple is that its author had no knowledge of the preceding story about Jesus' virginal conception. It seems to have circulated as a tradition independently of the Birth Narratives, designed as anticipatory of Jesus' future journey – as God's Son – from Galilee to Jerusalem.[130]

When Jesus quizzes the teachers in the Temple, he is portraying midrashically the story of Samuel who 'grew up in the presence of the Lord' (1 Samuel 2:21, cf. v.26 and 1 Samuel 3), referenced also in the earlier treatment of Jesus' Presentation in the Temple. Indeed, the story of Samuel, as midrash, informs much of the content of Luke 2. Once again, we are dealing not with history but with retrospective theology.

Zefirelli's superb film in its own way is an exercise in midrash, reflecting not so much events in the life of the historical Jesus but rather interpretations about the significance of his life, which continued to find (often bizarre) representation in the non-canonical gospels, typically the Gospel of Peter, with its strange account of a 'talking cross' accompanying Jesus when he rises from and leaves the tomb (vv.39–42).

There are seventeen known apocryphal gospels, two of which focus on childhood themes. The famous one is the Infancy Gospel of Thomas (IGT).[131] The other is the Protoevangelium of James (PoJ), about Mary.

parallels; cf. 14:58), and the truth it proclaims cannot be reduced to linear concepts of space and time.

Luke, following the hero motif, emphasises how the young Jesus continued to grow in wisdom, culminating with the pronouncement 'I must be in my Father's house', speaking in his own right, without the need for intermediaries – be they angels, dreams or human beings – and the canonical gospels go on to highlight his adult status by reference to miracles and preaching.[132]

IGT, however, pushes Jesus' miraculous deeds back into his childhood, typified by the Twelve Sparrows example that concluded the last chapter. The story is clearly absurd, yet it highlights the human tendency 'to find the man in the boy', reinforced by emphasising the wisdom theme, which is now so advanced that it intimidates Zacchaeus, Jesus' teacher, who has to appeal to Joseph: 'I have put myself to shame, taking on this child; he is not of this world, he can even tame fire. Maybe he was born before the world came into being. ... I was struggling to have a student, and now I have found a teacher' (7: 1-2).

Later, another teacher, having lost his temper, hits Jesus – he then curses the teacher, who falls dead. At this point, Joseph has Mary confine Jesus to their home, because 'those who anger him die'. They had good cause to be concerned – Jesus had also killed two of his fellow pupils (3:3, 4:1 and 14:2).

It is no surprise that this wunderkind was such a problem child. The purpose, however, of these legends is to emphasise Jesus' increasingly divine-like status, and they also point to the emerging chasm between Judaism and Christianity, symbolised by the ending of the Sparrows Story, when 'the Jew' reports Jesus' actions to 'their leaders' (2:5).

Richard Holloway identifies a possible remote historical context for some of these legendary stories – when Joseph, for example, yanks Jesus' ear for having killed yet another child (5:3). The child responds, 'I am not yours, stop annoying me'. It echoes 'I must be about my Father's business', and the synoptic gospels reflect apparent hostility between Jesus and his family, where they say that he is 'out of his mind' (Mark 3:21b and parallels).[133] Holloway suggests that all of these traditions may point to the psychological dissonance involved when people are 'forced' to choose between supposed mutually exclusive options.

This dissonance became more evident the longer Jesus' return was delayed, manifested spectacularly in the apocryphal gospels, which are really midrashim derived largely from the four canonical gospels.

Mary, as we have seen, also features in this apocryphal literature, most particularly in PoJ. Raymond Brown has noted there is no indication whatsoever that any New Testament author had an interest in Mary's marital relations after Jesus' birth. This concern is a later development, typified by the treatment of her in PoJ.[134]

Written c. 140 and attributed to James the brother of Jesus, scholars understand it to be the first known claim about Mary's perpetual virginity. PoJ influenced the eventual declaration of her as *Theotokos* (Mother of God) at Ephesus in 431. It is the site where Diana, goddess of the Moon and protector of women, had a temple. In time, this led to the Catholic doctrines of Mary's Immaculate Conception (1854) and Assumption (1950).

Mary's parents, Joachim and Anna, grateful to God for this late conception, dedicate her life (from age three) to virginal service in the Temple (PoJ 4:1b, 7:1). (It is of interest that Anna's pregnancy is confirmed by an angel whilst sitting beneath a laurel tree, reminiscent of how the Buddha's mother in labour was assisted by the drooping branches of a giant tree, attended by four angels.)

In the Temple, 'cared for like a dove', Mary received her food from the hand of an angel (8:1b). The angel's ministrations are a clear midrash on Jesus' Temptations in the Wilderness, when, after forty days of fasting, 'the Devil left him, and suddenly angels came and waited on him' (Matthew 4:11). Joachim also fasts for the same period of time (PoJ 1:4). There is no requirement to interpret 'forty days' in a literal sense. It is the Jewish way of saying 'a long time', with an obvious allusion to the Exodus from Egypt. Similarly, 'three days' means 'a short time'.

When Mary gives birth to Jesus, the midwife declares to Salome, 'A virgin has given birth, contrary to her natural condition', a claim Salome confirms by carrying out what nowadays would be called an obstetric examination (20:1). This verse, in the wider context of PoJ, is probably the basis for belief in Mary's perpetual virginity, which is how 20:1 came to be interpreted by some Christians by the end of the third century.

It is a mistake, however, to interpret these narratives, canonical or otherwise, as reporting real-time events. Their purpose is theological, not historical, and most certainly not biological. For the authors of the New Testament, 'the expression "death" – precisely like "birth" – does not have the matter-of-fact biological connotation that it has today – "birth" and "death" were mysteries, with an almost numinous character; and certainly there was no knowledge of conception in terms of later biology'.[135]

The infancy stories are undoubtedly 'mysterious' and 'numinous', and one of their leading protagonists – Joseph – had good cause to be mystified: 'Who has done this wicked deed in my home and defiled the virgin?', as PoJ expresses the matter (13:1b). It develops what we 'know' of him from its presumptive source in our two Infancy Narratives, especially Matthew's, which provides the only known 'biographical information' about Joseph.

Matthew relates three details:

- ▸ Joseph's father was named Jacob (1:16).
- ▸ God communicates with him through dreams (1:20, 2:13, 19 and 22).
- ▸ The role assigned to Joseph is to save Jesus by taking him south to Egypt.

This gospel's audience would have recognised these details. They are a midrash derived from the story of the patriarch Joseph (Genesis 37–50), whose father was also Jacob (35:24), and that Joseph was famous for his dreams: 'Look, I have had another dream: the sun, the moon and eleven stars were bowing down to me' (37:9, to give but one example).

What is most significant is that the patriarch Joseph's role in the drama of salvation was to save the people of the promise from death, by taking them down to Egypt (Genesis 45: 1–15) – 'God has made me lord of all Egypt; come down to me, do not delay' (v. 9b).[136]

Joseph of the Birth Stories has clearly been patterned on his namesake in Genesis. The character we identify as Jesus' earthly father is a recognisable literary device, similar to the Barabbas in the Passion Narratives.[137]

The touching nativity scene of Joseph on Christmas cards leading the pregnant Mary on a donkey to Bethlehem is an exercise in religious imagination, not history, and PoJ develops that sentimental tradition further. It has Joseph not leading the donkey but walking behind it. One of Joseph's sons by a supposed earlier marriage guides the donkey (17:2) and, in the region of Bethlehem, Joseph locates a cave for Mary to give birth (18:1), reminiscent of the legend about Mithras' birth.

This version of Joseph's role is a metaphor for his essential invisibility as part of the Jesus story, and it may be that, as a midrashic construct, Joseph served a function necessary in a patriarchal society, especially if there is any plausibility to the claim that a whiff of scandal may have surrounded Jesus' birth, hinted at when St John has the crowd say 'We were not born of fornication' (8:41).[138] It is probable that this verse gave rise to Celsus's polemical story about Panthera, the Roman legionary (see Chapter 2).

Arguments have been made that the apocryphal references to Joseph's sons actually relate to Jesus' siblings, some of whom are named by Mark in his gospel (6:3), but this hypothesis is difficult to sustain because there is no mention of them in the canonical Birth Narratives. The claim that these siblings may in fact be 'cousins' is likewise unlikely, for the simple reason that Greek has a discrete word for cousin – anepsios (see Colossians 4:10).

These ideas arise in the context of attempts to protect belief in Mary's perpetual virginity, which is contrary to the plain meaning of Mtatthew 1:24–25, 'Joseph ... took her as his wife, but had no marital relations with her until she had borne a son.'

It has been suggested that Mary, like Joseph, is a midrashic construct, but this hypothesis is a step too far, notwithstanding the virtual certainty that John's depiction of her at the foot of the cross is an exercise in pious imagination consistent with his theological vision (see 19: 25b–27).

There are good reasons for accepting that Mark's reference to Jesus as 'son of Mary' (6:3) preserves historical memories. Geza Vermes has remarked that the unusual appellation (rather than 'son of Joseph') is not as novel as some academics maintain, and that the synoptic gospels provide us with genuine insights into the ministry and teaching of the historical Jesus, providing we do not burden them with excessively literalist interpretations they cannot bear (that Jesus spoke the words attributed to him in Matthew 16:13–20, for example).

We need to remember that there is not a simple equivalence between the Gospel of Jesus and Jesus of the Gospels, no more than there is between the itinerant preacher who trod the pathways of Galilee and the great edifice of Christian dogma now bearing his 'signature'.

The two apocryphal infancy narratives also provide us with valuable insights, be they centred on a problem child or an ever virgin, but these insights have more to do with the psychology and sociology of religion than with its history.

In Place of a Conclusion

'When Rachel weeps, God listens.'

The Birth of Jesus the Jew (*BJJ*) attempts to show how the Infancy Narratives have everything to do with theology and nothing to do with biography or biology. It is reported that, a short time before his election to the papacy, Cardinal Ratzinger stated that 'relativity in truth' necessitates rigorous opposition if the Catholic Church's claim to be possessed of 'saving an unchanging truth' is to be preserved.[139]

It might be fairer to say that he understands the Church to be possessed by 'truth itself', but for all practical purposes the meaning is clear – the Magisterium of the Church, headed by the pope, exercising 'full, supreme and universal authority', is the authoritative body pertaining to the interpretation of divine revelation (see Catechism of the Catholic Church, nn. 874 to 896), which also claims that Jesus instituted the Church (n. 874).

Against this background, the Catechism and Cardinal Ratzinger, as he was then, aver that 'Jesus was born in a humble stable, into a poor family' (n. 525), and the context is clear that this is to be understood in a literal sense, as indeed is the one affirming Mary's 'real and perpetual virginity, even in the act of giving birth to the Son of God made man' (n. 499).

BJJ argues that the Birth Stories provide us with no historical information – they are genuine faith testimonies presented as biographical data. In other words, they are *haggadic midrashim*. It is what philosophers of language call a 'category error' to confuse midrash for historical information and, knowing what modern scholarship can demonstrate about the provenance of the Infancy Narratives, there is no requirement for us to persist in confusing the one with the other – thereby necessitating a revision of how doctrinal statements are to be understood, an urgent concern beyond the purview of this book.

Nobody ever asked Jesus the Jew about what is claimed in his name.[140]

Pope Emeritus Benedict's defence of 'unchanging truth' is really an excuse for not subjecting the doctrinal status quo to rigorous examination in the light of contemporary developments. The notion of 'unchanging truth' is a Platonic delusion and it has caused great harm, having contributed to the centuries-long Christian anti-Judaism, which, in turn, led indirectly to the Holocaust.

Human beings' apprehension of 'truth itself' changes all the time – 'relativity' is a constituent dimension of every word that has been uttered since the emergence of the cognitive revolution, about 70,000 years ago. As one scholar has eloquently remarked, 'We walk into the mystery of God; we do not define that mystery', and entering into the mystery is what the story of Christmas is all about.'[141]

Contrary to some anticipated objections, BJJ does not deny the truth of supernatural reality but rather seeks to situate God's providential guidance in the context of vibrant

IN PLACE OF A CONCLUSION

first-century Judaism. It incubated the birth of Christianity.

This book will not be to the liking of many Christians, and Catholics in particular may object to it on the grounds, to paraphrase Hubert Richards, that one can get away with suggesting things about Jesus but Our Lady is a no-go area, because concerning her believers experience 'an emotional involvement which makes them far more ready to take offence, and be far less open to discussion'.[142]

Richards quotes from Brendan Behan's masterpiece, *Borstal Boy*:

> The day I made my First Communion I had prayed to God to take me, as Napoleon prayed, when I would go straight to Heaven. ... I had never given up the Faith (what would I give it up for?), and now I was glad that even in this smelly English hell-hole of Victorian cruelty, ... I would be at one with hundreds of millions of Catholics, at the Sacrifice of the Mass, and to pray to Our Lady, the Mother of God and of man.[143]

For Behan, observes Richards, 'Mass was identified with praying to Our Lady', and it situates the challenge when discussions about the Virgin Mary encompass theological investigation. Behan's 'involvement' with the Virgin Mary conflicts with how Jewish tradition understands her, as a mother who conceived Jesus naturally and perhaps illicitly.

There is a danger that legitimate historical enquiry is drowned out by appeals to the preservation of 'simple faith'. This consideration is beyond the scope of this book, but there is urgent need for the mainline churches to address it.

Jacob Neusner argues that the only way for Jews to understand Christianity is within Jewish terms and the only way for Christians to understand Judaism is within Christian terms. He means that, despite Christianity's origins in Judaism, we must now recognise that the two religions are utterly distinct, and it is against this background that 'the work of attempting a dialogue can begin'.[144]

Neusner suggests that the figure of the Virgin Mary has a role in furthering that dialogue, recognising – as exemplified by Borstal Boy – that she is 'the bearer of profound religious sentiments'. He believes that the story of the Flight into Egypt, examined in Chapter 7, provides a point of genuine contact between Catholicism and Judaism, because 'Mary is a figure much like Rachel, protecting her children and weeping for them'.[145]

The Flight into Egypt is represented as 'a counterpart to the Exile of Israel in the time of Jeremiah. Mary stands for Rachel and Jesus for Jeremiah'. In his reading of the Hebrew Bible, Neusner has found in Rachel – weeping for her children in Ramah – a figure that incorporates many of the traits Catholics like Behan attribute to Mary. She is 'a woman who bears a special, a unique, relationship to God, a relationship so compelling that he will respond to Mary in a way that God will not respond to any other person.'[146]

For many Catholics, Mary's prayers carry more weight than any man's, and in Rachel Neusner identifies a figure who intercedes and intervenes for Jews in a manner similar to how Mary mediates between God and Catholics. Jews, he acknowledges, seldom make such connections, but Neusner's point is that, when Rachel is understood in relation to her unique role in Judaism, she triumphs – like Mary – when all other interventions falter. She succeeds where Abraham, Isaac, Jacob and Moses fail to relate to God in terms of familial love. He listens to mothers and responds to their pleas: 'When Rachel weeps, God listens'.

IN PLACE OF A CONCLUSION

Neusner cannot relate to Catholicism's doctrinal version of Jesus, maintaining that it is 'wholly other' for Jews, but he can identify with Mary, who echoes Rachel's intercession for her children, and by so doing Neusner believes that Catholics and Jews, together for all that separates them, have found a way of honouring the living God.

This book, written in the shadows cast by the Holocaust, is a modest contribution to honouring that vision of realising a shared Catholic-Jewish narrative, one rooted in respect for, and celebration of, the dignity of difference, because God has no favourites.

David Hume (d. 1776), of Scottish Enlightenment renown, famously remarked: 'A wise man proportions his belief to the evidence.' The evidence tells us that the Infancy Narratives are constituted exclusively of haggadic midrashim, exemplified in particular by Matthew 1:23's misuse of Isaiah 7:14.

Jesus was unaware of these narratives, as was St Paul, our first 'Christian writer', whose gospel was about 'the Christ'. The Apostle to the Gentiles had no knowledge of, and probably little interest in, Jesus the Jew, born in Nazareth, apart from the (atonement) significance he attributed to Jesus' death.

This concept is Christianity's problematic foundation stone and the Infancy Gospels assume it, despite no star hovering over Bethlehem; yet this fact should not deter us from celebrating the spiritual reality that the Christmas Story addresses the deepest yearnings of our hearts, animating 'the hope that is within us' (Colossians 1:5). It also provides us with an important key to unlocking the wonder of midrash.

Endnotes

Dedication

1. Robert Funk, Honest To Jesus: Jesus For A new Millennium (HTJ, Harper, 1996 edition, page 300); Chapter 4 of this book, 'Heroes of Divine Origin', is derived from Funk's Chapter 15, 'The Divine Child', as is the distinction between 'the Gospel of Jesus' and 'the Jesus of the Gospels'. Jesus the Jew, a term which will be used throughout this book, is the title of Geza Vermes' ground-breaking work (Collins, 1973).

Chapter 1

2. John Dominic Crossan, Jesus: A Revolutionary Biography (JRB, Harper One, 1994 edition, page 158).
3. Sourced and adapted from Shadows of Auschwitz: A Christian Response to the Holocaust, Harry J. Cargas (SoA, Crossroad Publishing, 1990 edition, page 15, slightly edited without alteration of meaning).
4. Ibid., page 16, quoted from Irving Greenberg's Judaism and Christianity after the Holocaust (Journal of Ecumenical Studies, Issue 12, 1975, page 526) – it is important to emphasise that many other Catholic prelates disapproved of such views and actively helped to save Jews during the war.

5   The First Christmas – What Really Happened? (TFC1 – Collins, Fontana Books, 1973, page 18)

6   Ibid.

7   Ibid., page 19.

8   A different interpretation is provided by the Catechism of the Catholic Church, n. 498 and, technically, Matthew does provide at least one piece of historical information, corroborated by secular sources: the death of Herod the Great (probably 4 BCE). And see Note 62, below.

9   For a comprehensive treatment of this interpretation of the data, see Thomas Sheehan's The First Coming – How the Kingdom of God Became Christianity (TFCK, Random House, 1998 edition, pages 192– 205).

10   Karen Armstrong, The Case for God – What Religion Really Means (The Bodley Head, 2009 edition, page 89).

11   John Shelby Spong, Biblical Literalism: A Gentile Heresy (BLH, Harper Collins, 2017 edition).

12   Sheehan, an extrapolation from the chart on page 194.

13   Beyond the Quest for the Historical Jesus – Memoir of a Discovery (MoD, Sheffield Phoenix Press, 2012 edition, page 41.

14   The Book of the People – How to read the Bible (BoP, Atlantic Books, 2015 edition, page 169).

15   MoD, page 231.

16   John Shelby Spong's Jesus for the non-Religious (JNR, Harper Collins, 2007 edition, pages 97–105) is typical of convincing academic support for these and related claims.

17   Ibid, page 156, referencing also the previous paragraph.

18   The New Jerusalem Bible (NJBC, Geoffrey Chapman, 1991 edition, page 672) – Matthew 27:25, known as The Blood

Cry, is the most notorious verse in the New Testament. The crowd never said any such thing, and Viviano has explained how it is a midrash derived from various sources: 1 Kings 2:33, 2 Samuel 1:16, Jeremiah 26:15 and 51:35. It is interesting that Matthew 27:25 does not include a 'forever' clause, unlike 1 Kings 2:33. We are best understanding the verse against the background that ensued after the Great Jewish-Roman War.

19   This paragraph is much adapted from BoP, page 157.

Chapter 2

20   Red Stripe Press, 2020 edition, page X – Teilhard's two other observations are that Catholicism excludes democracy and marginalises women in its articulation of the Christian proclamation.

21   For a contrary view, see Raymond Brown, The Birth of the Messiah (BoM, Doubleday, 1993 edition, pages 516–23). 'Mark' is the first of our four (canonical) gospels.

22   The point is that Bethlehem became the traditional birthplace of Jesus once his Messianic status was being championed by Gentile Jewish-Christianity, from c. 80.

23   Paul, Rabbi and Apostle (Augsburg, 1984, page 47).

24   Geza Vermes, Christian Beginnings (Penguin Group, 2012 edition, Chapter 4) provides detailed and convincing arguments for this position.

25   This book does not address the notoriously complex ontological and psychological issues pertinent to the relationship between 'Jesus' and 'the Christ', save to remark that, in the shadows cast the Holocaust, that 'dynamic' requires urgent attention.

26   Texts, Contexts and Cultures: Essays on Biblical Topics

(Veritas, 2002 edition, page 129).

27   The Jewish Annotated New Testament (JANT, Oxford University Press, 2017 edition, page 245).

28   Ibid.

29   Adapted from TFC1, page 22.

30   This paragraph is much adapted from John Barton's A History of the Bible – The Book and its Faiths (HoB, Penguin Books, 2019 edition, page 319).

31   Ibid. Barton is summarising arguments of R. Kendall Soulen, in his The God of Israel and Christian Theology (Fortress Press, 1996).

Chapter 3

32   The Dignity of Difference (DoD, Continuum, 2002 edition, page 53, slightly adapted).

33   JANT, page 111.

34   Hyam Maccoby's The Mythmaker: Paul and the Invention of Christianity (Weidenfeld & Nicholson, 1986 edition) addresses this controversial interpretation of the Ebionites (a probable nickname meaning 'the poor ones') in comprehensive detail, particularly Chapter 15.

35   There are also translations into Aramaic.

36   This paragraph and the succeeding two are sourced and adapted from BLH, pages 68–69.

37   The Story of the Jews: Finding the Words – 1000 BCE to 1492 CE (SoJ, Random House, 2013 edition, page 151).

38   BLH, page 69.

39   Nativity, Passion and Resurrection (NPR, Penguin Books, 2010 one-volume edition, page 70).

40   This sentence and its preceding short paragraphs are

sourced from CFJ and Vermes's NPR, page 69.

41 Mark L. Strauss, Four Portraits, one Jesus (FPJ, Zonerdam, 2007 edition, page 415).

42 NPR, page 69.

43 Ibid. In his ground-breaking Jesus the Jew (JtJ, Collins, 1973, page 214), Vermes had adopted the position, later revised, that Is. 7:14 is more satisfactorily explained 'as an endeavour to justify scripturally an otherwise inexplicable tradition, rather than as its source.

44 BoM, page 146, much abridged and adapted without alteration in meaning.

45 Ibid. Brown's reference is to the virginal conception, not to 'Waco', which is employed as an extreme illustration of how 'prophecy' can be misunderstood – there is no intention to imply a moral equivalence between how 'Luke' and 'Matthew' used 'Bethlehem' and what transpired at 'Waco'.

46 Ibid.

47 Ibid.

48 NPR, page 79.

49 Ibid.

50 Ibid., page 78. Vermes offers a detailed analysis of his thesis, explaining how, for instance, Mary's reply to the Angel Gabriel (1:34) is 'odd' in the context of Judaism at that time.

51 Ibid, paged 80, Mirabile Dictu means literally 'wonderful to relate'.

52 JtJ, page 221.

53 Ibid, page 222.

54 Hilde Brekke-Moller, in The Vermes Quest: The Signif-

icance of Geza Vermes for Jesus Research (TVQ, T&T Clark, 2017 edition, pages 65–66). Leander Keck, in a critique of Jesus the Jew makes the 'unnecessary observation'; Freyne's observation is indirectly related to it (see TVQ, pages 230 and 232 for bibliographical references).

55 Penguin Books (2000 edition, page 263).

56 Mark 6:3, cf. Matthew13: 55–56.

57 Tortuous arguments are made by Evangelical Christians and others to square this proverbial circle, but they lack credibility for many reasons, and not least because textual analysis of how the New Testament was composed confirms that the Infancy Narratives reflect, and do not precede, its developing theology about the person of Jesus. Mainline Catholic and Protestant scholarship far better understands the situation: it is possible to adhere to the doctrine of the virginal conception without having to rely exclusively upon the New Testament (see also Note 62, below).

58 This paragraph is adapted from John Macquarrie's Principles of Christian Theology (PCT, SCM Press, 1977 edition, page 280).

59 In his voluminous writings, Brown rejected utterly simplistic interpretations of the Bible, but he nonetheless argued that, on doctrinal grounds, it is possible to reconcile the findings of modern scholarship about these narratives with belief in Jesus' virginal conception. Of this approach, Vermes has written, 'Brown recognises that angelic appearances, virginal conception and the marvellous star are "patently legendary themes", that Matthew and Luke contradict each other, and that neither account is likely to be historical. But when it comes to the crunch, he opts for what he admits to be a "retrogressively con-

servative" position, and is willing to shock his progressive critics even more by affirming that it is easier to explain the New Testament evidence of the virginal conception by postulating a historical basis for it than by accepting it as pure theological creation'. Vermes claims that it is no surprise that, reviewing The Birth of the Messiah ... , Frank Kermode, in the New York Review of Books, has attributed Brown's refusal to acknowledge the made-up character of Matthew's birth story to Brown's eagerness 'to secure the Catholic Church's imprimatur for his book', concluding with the sardonic observation: 'Giving up the Virgin Birth might be bad for people' (NPR, pages 21–22 and page 445), and see Notes 9, above, and 76, below.

60 HTJ, page 281. Funk dates the Infancy Narratives to the early second century.

Chapter 4

61 Ibid., page 282.
62 Ibid. Mc Gaughey's book is Infancy Narratives in the Ancient World (1992 edition, adapted), quoted by Funk, page 282.
63 Ronald Brownrigg, Who's Who – The New Testament (WWNT, Weidenfeld and Nicholson, 1993 edition, pages 252 to 253), the practice was by no means universal in the 'Paganisms' of the Ancient Near East.
64 JANT, page 14.
65 HtJ, page 283.
66 Ibid.
67 Ibid., page 284, adapted.
68 Ibid., much adapted.
69 Ibid., page 281.

70 This paragraph and the three preceding ones are loosely sourced from Barrie Wilson's How Jesus Became Christian (JBC, Weidenfeld and Nicolson, 2008 edition, pages 219–221). On page 229, he makes this challenging observation: 'In many ways, in practice, Christians since Marcion have been Marcionites, despite official Church pronouncements to the contrary.'

71 BoM, page 523.

72 Ibid.

73 Ibid., page 524. In The Virginal Conception & Bodily Resurrection of Jesus (VCB, Paulist Pres 1973 edition,), Brown discusses the 'evidence' in great detail, concluding that 'the totality of the scientifically-controllable evidence leaves an unresolved problem' (page 66), implying that affirming belief in Jesus' virginal conception can be settled only by reference to Church teaching (see Catechism of the Catholic Church, n. 498, and Notes 9 and 62, above).

74 JBC, pages 208 and 209.

75 John Dominic Crossan, How to Read the Bible & Still Be A Christian (HtRB, Harper Collins, 1989 edition, page 18).

76 Ibid., page 209.

77 TFC1, page 24.

78 Ibid., page 25.

Chapter 5

79 Ibid., pages 65 to 66, much adapted, and referencing the 'goggle in amazement' quotation of the previous paragraph.

80 Ibid., page 45.

81 JnR, page 19.

82 Ibid.
83 Marcus Borg and Dominic Crossan, The First Christmas: What the Gospels Really Teach About Jesus' Birth (TFC2, SPCK, 2008 edition, page 173, and the preceding two paragraphs are much adapted from TFC2).
84 Ibid., page 172. This paragraph was written on a day in January 2021 when close friends of mine had their first grandchild, and there is already more official information, digital and otherwise, in existence about her than there ever was regarding 99.999% of the population of the Roman Empire.
85 Ibid., adapted.
86 Ibid., much adapted, with reference also to the preceding paragraph.
87 An Introduction to the New Testament (INT, Doubleday, 1996 edition, page 176, adapted).
88 TFC2, pages 181–82, adapted.
89 JnR, page 18. Much of the material on the Three Kings derives from this book.
90 NPR, page 112.
91 TFC2, page 165, abridged.
92 Ibid., page 166, slightly adapted.
93 WWNT, page 227. However, this 'presence' should not be interpreted to mean that women of the period were enrolled for tax or voting purposes (see JnR, page 23).
94 Bloomsbury, 2013 edition, page 42.
95 JnR, page 22.
96 Ibid.
97 Ibid., page 23.
98 Ibid., page 23.

99 Ibid., much adapted.

100 NJBC, page 683.

101 Ibid.

102 Ibid. Interested readers are referred to Karris' argument, referenced on page 683.

103 NJBC, page 683.

104 Ibid.

Chapter 6

105 TFC1, page 28, adapted.

106 Karen Armstrong, A Short History of Myth (SHM, Canongate, 2005 edition, page 106, much adapted).

107 TFC1, pages 27–28.

108 Jeremy Cohen, Christ Killers – The Jews and the Passion, From the Bible to the Big Screen (CK, Oxford University Press, 2007 edition, pages 95–102) provides a fascinating account of this extraordinary story.

109 Ibid., page 95.

110 Ibid., pages 94 and 98.

111 Ibid., page 100, page 102 discusses the possibility that it may have originated in the German town of Würzburg.

112 Ibid., page 102.

113 Ibid., pages 100 and 268 (it provides online confirmation, as of 3 August 2005).

114 Ena Gray, Healing the Past – Catholic anti-Semitism: Roots and Redemption (HtP, Veritas, 2009 edition, page 115).

115 Ibid.

116 Ibid., pages 116 to 117.

117 Herod was a very complex individual, and this book – for obvious reasons – emphasises his negative character traits. Readers who are interested in learning more about this extraordinary man are referred to Geza Vermes' last book (published posthumously by Bloomsbury, 2014): The True Herod.

118 NPR, page 120.

119 TFC 2, page 144, much abridged and adapted.

120 Ibid., adapted.

121 Ibid., page 136.

122 Ibid., pages 137–138, adapted.

123 Ibid.

124 Ibid., much adapted.

125 Ibid. Cyrus had defeated the Babylonians.

126 BoM, page 215 – in NJBC, noting further that 'Matthew's story would not be fantastic to the readers who knew the history of Herodian times' (page 228). The NJBC (Brown is one of its editors) argues that 'the story may not be historical but possesses verisimilitude' (page 636). It also makes the point that 'Matthew wishes to associate Jesus with Jeremiah as the suffering prophet of the New Covenant (Matthew 26:28, cf. Jeremiah 31: 31–34). And see Note 62, above.

127 NPR, page 117.

128 From Jesus to Christ – The origins of the New Testament: Images of Jesus (Yale University Press, 1988 edition, page 38).

129 Infancy Gospel of Thomas 2: 2–4, from Bart D. Ehrman's Lost Scriptures (Oxford University Press, 2003 edition, page 58)

Chapter 7

130 NJBC, page 684.

131 IGT is often confused with the Gospel of Thomas (GoT), discovered at Nag Hammadi in 1945. The former is dated to the early second century and GoT to a similar time, reflecting at least some of its Gnostic themes (the Gospel has 114 'sayings' attributed to Jesus, some of which reflect material in the canonical gospels). Interested readers are referred to Bart D. Ehrman's Lost Scriptures – Books that did not make it into the New Testament (LS, Oxford University Press, 2003 edition) for a comprehensive introduction to the Apocryphal Writings.

132 NJBC, page 684, adapted.

133 The Good Book (TGB, Granta Publications, 2006 edition – most of the material on the possible relationship between IGT and the synoptic gospels derives from pages 68–71). Other references are Mark 3:25, 6:3 and John 7:5.

134 BoM, pages 305–06 and interpreted in the light of Holloway's suggestion.

135 PCT, page 281.

136 JNR, page 32, adapted.

137 Ibid., page 33, adapted.

138 Ibid., page 31, much adapted.

139 Quoted in BLH, page 197.

Conclusion

140 Christian theologians of systematic theology have sophisticated answers to this 'challenge', which may or may not be convincing. My point is that we need to return not so much to 'what really happened' in the first and second centuries – an unrealistic expectation – but to a Christian

theology rooted far more in an appreciation of the person of the historical Jesus, with less emphasis on him as 'the Christ', which I readily acknowledge to be far from easy, and millions of Christians regard it as unnecessary.

141 Ibid., page 140, much redacted.
142 TFC1, page 100.
143 Ibid., page 101.
144 Jews and Christians: The Myth of a Common Tradition (JCM, SCM Press, 1991 edition, page 120.
145 Ibid., page 122.
146 Ibid., page 123.

Related books

The Outlaw Christ
JOHN F. DEAN

(Columba Books, Paperback, €16.99) ISBN 9781782183662

Poets throughout the years have taken up the message and person of Jesus. Often, in the side-lining or the outlawing of Christ, the poets, too, have been 'Outlawed'.

The Outlaw Christ is a stimulating and intriguing anthology of poems that bring Christ to life in our own uncertain and challenging times.Developed from a series of talks and lectures at Loyola University, Chicago, follows the poets like John Donne, George Herbert, Gerard Manley Hopkins, Patrick Kavanagh, Pádraig J. Daly and James Harpur among others in their search for the true Christ.

Voices from the Desert. The Lost Legacy of the Skelligs
HUGH MACMAHON

(Columba Books, Paperback, €14.99) ISBN 9781782183808

In 384 AD, John Cassian began his 24 interviews with famous Desert Fathers and recorded them in *The Conferences* which had a profound effect on spiritual life in Western Europe, especially in Ireland.

Voices from the Desert presents an authentic understanding of Christianity separate from the institutional and theological prisms that came later. Individuals looking for a fresh view of what it means to be a Christian, or to understand the Skelligs' legacy, will appreciate its authenticity, clarity and relevance.

ALL BOOKS ARE AVAILABLE TO ORDER DIRECTLY FROM
WWW.COLUMBABOOKS.COM

Want to keep reading?

Columba Books has a whole range of books to inspire your faith and spirituality.

As the leading independent publisher of religious and theological books in Ireland, we publish across a broad range of areas including pastoral resources, spirituality, theology, the arts and history.

All our books are available through
www.columbabooks.com
and you can find us on Twitter, Facebook and Instagram to discover more of our fantastic range of books. You can sign up to our newletter through the website for the latest news about events, sales and to keep up to date with our new releases.

@columbabooks

@ColumbaBooks

columba_books